International Monetary Policy after the Euro

This volume is dedicated to our wives,
Valerie Mundell, Lori Zak, and Chelsea Schaeffer.

International Monetary Policy after the Euro

Edited by

Robert A. Mundell

Professor, Columbia University, US

Paul J. Zak

Associate Professor of Economics and Director, Center for Neuroeconomics Studies, Claremont Graduate University, US

Derek M. Schaeffer

Doctoral Candidate (Economics) Claremont Graduate University, US

Edward Elgar

Cheltenham, UK • Northampton, MA, USA

Published by
Edward Elgar Publishing Limited
Glensanda House
Montpellier Parade
Cheltenham
Glos GL50 1UA
UK

Edward Elgar Publishing, Inc.
136 West Street
Suite 202
Northampton
Massachusetts 01060
USA

A catalogue record for this book
is available from the British Library

Library of Congress Cataloguing in Publication Data
Bologna–Claremont International Monetary Conference (16th : 2000 :
  Bologna, Italy)
   International monetary policy after the euro / edited by Robert A.
Mundell, Paul J. Zak, Derek M. Schaeffer.
       p. cm.
   "Proceedings of the Bologna–Claremont conference held in March 23–25,
2000 at the Johns Hopkins Center in Bologna, Italy"—Intro.
   1. Monetary policy—Congresses. 2. Euro—Congresses. 3. International
finance—Congresses. 4. Euro area—Congresses. I. Mundell, Robert A. II.
Zak, Paul J. III. Schaeffer, Derek M. IV. Title.

HG230.3.B655 2000
339.5'3—dc22

                                                                2004057461

ISBN   1 84542 121 3

Printed and bound in Great Britain by MPG Books Ltd, Bodmin, Cornwall

Contents

Contributors

Mate Babic, Professor, University of Zagreb, Croatia
Mario Baldassarri, Professor, University of Rome 'La Sapienza', Italy
Robert Bartley, Editor, *Wall Street Journal*, USA
Giorgio Basevi, Professor, University of Bologna, Italy
Richard Blackhurst, Professor, Graduate Institute of International Studies, Geneva, Switzerland
Emil Maria Claassen, Professor, University of Paris-Dauphine, France
Richard Clarida, Professor, Columbia University, USA
Armand Clesse, Director, Luxembourg Institute for European and International Studies, Luxembourg
Richard Cooper, Professor, Harvard University, USA
W. Max Corden, Professor, The Johns Hopkins University, USA
Robert H. Evans, Director, The Johns Hopkins University Bologna Center, Italy
Paul Fabra, Director General, Centre for the New Europe, Belgium
Herbert Giersch, Professor, Kiel Institute, Germany
Enzo Grilli, AGIP Professor in International Economics, The Johns Hopkins Bologna Center, Italy
Otmar Issing, Chief Economist, European Central Bank, Germany
Christopher Johnson, Investment Counsellor, United Kingdom
Václav Klaus, former Prime Minister of the Czech Republic
Nicolas Krul, Consultant, Switzerland
Alexandre Lamfalussy, former President, European Monetary Institute, Germany
Axel Leijonhufvud, Professor, University of California Los Angeles, USA, and University of Trento, Italy
Massimiliano Marzo, University of Bologna and The Johns Hopkins Bologna Center, Italy
Robert A. Mundell, 1999 Nobel Laureate in Economics and Professor, Columbia University, USA

Manfred Neumann, Director, Institute for International Political Economy, University of Bonn, Germany

Robert Pringle, Corporate Director for Public Policy and Research, World Gold Council, United Kingdom

Lord Robert Skidelsky, Professor, University of Warwick, United Kingdom

André Szász, former Minister of Finance, The Netherlands

Niels Thygesen, Professor, University of Copenhagen, Denmark

Paul Volcker, former Federal Reserve Board Chairman, USA

Norbert Walter, Chief Economist, Deutsche Bank Group, Germany

Paul J. Zak, Associate Professor of Economics and Director, Center for Neuroeconomics Studies, Claremont Graduate University, USA

Foreword

By

Robert H. Evans

When the sixteenth Bologna Center–Claremont Graduate University Monetary Conference was held in Bologna in Spring 2000 the world was a different one. The bubble had not burst, corporate mergers were still fashionable, a major conflict did not rage, the Middle East was seemingly in equilibrium, and the price of petroleum was stable.

The conference focused on the management of major currency exchange movements. And prophetic it was. Currency fluctuations have reached critical levels as the euro strengthened over 40 percent since its introduction in relation to the dollar, affecting not only tourists' pocket books but also the development and expansion of European economies.

Matters were certainly simpler when in 1967, C. Grove Haines, with the support of the World Gold Council, launched the first conference; gold was the central focus of discussion. In 2001, once again the World Gold Council made our meeting possible, and thanks go to its Managing Director of Public Policy and Research, Robert Pringle.

The major characteristic, the spirit, of the previous meetings – free-flowing discussion among distinguished economists, often challenged by "Young Turks" – is respected in this book which addresses, effectively, the issue of major currency exchange rate movements in a context of even greater capital flows. The issue of the future of the international monetary system is still open – as we knew it would be when we convened.

While I left the Bologna Center in Summer 2003, the subject of the conference remained in my thoughts as I now administer the American University of Rome which until recently had income in dollars and expenses in euros!

1.   Introduction

By

Robert A. Mundell and Paul J. Zak

For more than three decades, the Bologna–Claremont Monetary Conferences have generated lively and engaging debates on international monetary policy. Academics, bankers and officials from all over the world have discussed the most important issues at the forefront of international monetary policy and debated prospects for reform. This volume reports the proceedings of the Bologna–Claremont conference held in March 23–25, 2000 at the Johns Hopkins Center in Bologna, Italy.

The first conference of the series was held at the Bologna Center in 1967. Its inspiration stemmed from the problems arising from the precarious state of the gold-anchored fixed exchange rate international monetary system that had served the world economy in the post-war decades. Major exchange rates were fixed to the US dollar, which in turn was convertible into gold. But price levels in all the major countries had soared during and after World War II, the Korean War and the Vietnam War, while the dollar price of gold had been maintained at $35 an ounce, originally set at this rate in 1934. As gold became scarce, countries turned to using dollar balances in lieu of gold for international payments and reserves. But the buildup of dollar balances created new problems as its convertibility into gold became increasingly questionable. Shifts in central bank portfolios led to a drain on the US gold stock and speculation, putting the international monetary system in jeopardy. The international monetary system seemed to be stuck on the horns of a dilemma, first identified by the Belgian economist, Professor Robert Triffin of Yale University: If the US did not correct its balance of payments deficit, there would be a convertibility crisis; but if it did correct it, the world would run short of reserves and bring on global deflation like that in the 1930s. The system did break down, and the failure to find a way to negotiate a restoration of the system led to the ratification of a regime of fluctuating exchange rates in the 1970s.

Fluctuating exchange rates of course did not solve the inherent problems of the system. Under fluctuating exchange rates, the dollar retained a key role in international payments as unit of account, invoice, intervention, and reserve currency. Problems of the US deficit were replaced by problems arising from the dollar cycle. The weak dollar of the late 1970s was replaced by the strong dollar of the early 1980s and the weak dollar of the early 1990s, only to be replaced again by the strong dollar associated with the IT revolution and the weak dollar of the global slowdown that started at the end of the decade. Over much of this period, many countries resented the unique role of the dollar in the system and worked to create zones of fixed exchange rates outside the dollar area. The most spectacular of these new currency areas is the euro area. The euro came into being in 1999 and was a major issue of discussion at the Bologna conference and is so in this book.

The advent of the euro was, arguably, one of the most important monetary events of the twentieth century. With its very creation it became the second most important currency in the world. Within the euro area, it gave every individual a more important currency than he or she had before, every firm a global capital market, every country lower interest rates and it created for the monetary area as a whole a purchasing power parity area that had been only partial even under fixed exchange rates. For the world as a whole it created an alternative to the dollar in case the dollar became unstable and an alternative global currency in which to hold foreign exchange reserves. Perhaps most important of all, it created a change in the power configuration of the system, a movement away from a polarized world economy dependent on the dollar to a multipolar world of large competing currency areas.

In recent years the three largest currency areas – the dollar, euro and yen areas – have been characterized by a remarkable degree of price stability coupled, paradoxically, with a high degree of volatility and even instability of the major exchange rates. Unfortunately, with increased decentralization of power, there has been a noticeable absence of leadership stressing the need for cooperation and multilateral management of interdependence. One issue that arises again and again is whether there is any possibility of creating a truly global currency along the lines of the early American and British plans prepared for discussion at the Bretton Woods conference 60 years ago. Paul Volcker, the eminent Chairman of the Federal Reserve System in the 1980s has argued persuasively that "the global economy needs a global currency." Whether or not that is a possible or likely prospect is a subject that is likely to be with us far into the new century.

Over the years the Bologna–Claremont conferences have hotly debated such issues as fixed versus floating exchange rates, the gold standard, management (or mismanagement) of international crises in Mexico, Asia and Russia, economic development of the poorest countries, US economic leadership, the rise of Europe as a unified economic power, the rise of China, the role and functioning of the International Monetary Fund, the international debt crisis and sundry other topics. These analyses brought out sharp areas of disagreement as well as considerable consensus, reflecting the state of dissent in the economics profession at large. The proceedings of the conference reported here follow the same format that permits issues to be dissected, debated, analysed and re-analysed until, often, a consensus is reached. Even if a consensus is not reached, there is enough analysis so that the reader can choose sides or draw his or her own conclusions!

As time passes, a toll has been taken on many of our participants. The earliest conferences included famous economists like Lord Robbins, Robert Triffin, Edward Bernstein, James Meade, Jacques Rueff, Lord Kaldor and Marcus Fleming, all of whom have passed away. A particularly great loss was Randall Hinshaw who was offered and willingly accepted the difficult task of editing the conference series, a job he fulfilled with a dedication, sensitivity, skill and love that has, we think, been unrivalled in the history of economic conferences.

This conference may well be the last in the series, and it is fitting that its theme allowed us to look at the prospects for the evolution of monetary institutions for the new century. The dialog shows, however, that the ultimate form monetary arrangements will take in the twenty-first century is anything but a settled issue. The set of possibilities ranges from a single world currency, to a world with three currency blocks, to a large number of currencies pegged to two or three major currencies, to a large number of floating currencies. The benefits and costs of the alternatives are discussed at some length.

Management of the interdependence implied by large current account imbalances will pose new challenges for international monetary cooperation in the future. It is our hope that the dialog in this book will contribute to a better understanding of international monetary issues and stimulate much-needed new thinking on the subject.

Thanks are due to Tom Brayton of Claremont who transcribed the proceedings, Gabriella Chiaporri in Bologna for excellent organizing assistance, and Robert Evans, Director of the Bologna Center, for arranging the conference. Financial support for the production of this volume was provided by the European Union Center of California by Professor David Andrews.

2.   Issues facing the global economy

Introduced by

Robert H. Evans

ROBERT EVANS: Welcome to the 16th edition of the Bologna–Claremont Monetary Conference. The conference started back in 1967, when Seagrove Haynes was the director of the [John Hopkins University Bologna] Center and [Claremont Graduate University economist] Randall Hinshaw was a visiting professor. The very first conference, I believe, focused on gold and the role of gold in the international monetary system. Today, your reflections will emphasize the euro, the dollar and the future of the international monetary system. I'm sure the discussions that will take place around this table will be as stimulating as those of the many conferences that have preceded it. As you know, Bob Mundell has coordinated the program and I want to thank him very much for all his efforts.

The idea is to have a free-flowing dialogue amongst participants. The principal change, because change does occur in the Bologna–Claremont Conferences, means that this year we will have two lectures rather than one: the Lord Robbins Memorial Lecture and the Randall Hinshaw Memorial Lecture. As I look around the table, I see a good number of people whom I would call the stalwarts of this conference, but I also see a good number of new faces, which is excellent. We need to always bring in new ideas and new participants. We miss a few of our traditional participants, some Nobel Prize winners who have participated in past conferences. Age, a few operations, and things of the sort have slowed them down. There is one person I would like to mention because this conference was on his agenda, the late Clyde Mujyakumsen. As a friend and Bologna Center alumnus, his participation in these discussions will be sorely missed. We all look forward to the discussions that are going to take place, the staff, faculty and especially the students, because this conference has a double purpose – it is primarily geared toward the participants, but it is also for the students and the alumni, who wish to keep up with people who are doing economics.

Conferences of this kind could only take place because we have friends. Since the academic enterprise only forges ahead with the support of others – those who in the recent years have helped us endow a Chair in German Studies, those who have helped us create the Adjunct Chair in International Economics, which next year will be held by our friend Robert Mundell, and I think it is totally appropriate that he be the occupant, because so much of the work for which he received the Nobel Prize was conceived and written here in the late 1950s, early 1960s. And Bob, in [MIT economist and 1970 Nobel Laureate] Paul Samuelson's words, was then the best-looking contemporary economist. Today, he remains the best-looking practicing economist, and we're really glad that he is here, not only for his looks, but especially for his work and his spirit that has animated this conference. So to all of you, welcome to the School of Advanced International Studies, welcome to the Bologna Center, and welcome to Bologna, the European capital of culture for the year 2000. I am delighted you are here, and I very sincerely wish you a stimulating two days of dialogue.

ROBERT MUNDELL: Thank you, Robert. I want to just second your remarks about our regrets at not having Clyde [Mujyakumsen] here. When I first came to the Bologna Center in 1959 we became good friends and he has played a role in so many conferences that we have attended together; we will very much miss him here. A couple of words about the first conference in 1967. For those who were not here, it was actually sponsored in part by the Chamber of Mines of South Africa. We included a discussion of gold, of course, because gold was at the center of the international monetary system. But what was remarkable about that first conference was that it was moderated by Lord Robbins, who came to all of the conferences that he could. However, it also included people like [Yale economist] Robert Triffin, [former IMF Research Director and Brookings economist] Eddie Bernstein, [Oxford economist] Sir Roy Heard, and [Cambridge economist and 1977 Nobel Laureate] James Meade.

At the first conference people were talking about reform of the international monetary system. This was very much in the air at the time because the US was running short of gold and nobody wanted to bring about a recurrence of deflation with everyone trying to compete for gold in the world. The dollar and the US balance of payments deficit were also problems that were very much on the minds of people. Plans for reform were rife when Jacques Rueff wanted to double the price of gold. He turned on the gold standard and he had the considerable backing of General de Gaulle. Robert Triffin, picking up on the Cannes plan of 1944, wanted a world central bank. Eddie Bernstein, who was the first director of research at the IMF, wanted a reserve asset. Later, James Meade and [Chicago economist and 1976 Nobel Laureate] Milton Friedman advocated flexible exchange rates. So the first conference had all of the principal authors of the major plans and that got the Bologna Center series off to a grand start. We were so fortunate in having Randall Hinshaw teaching that year at the Bologna Center and he was the ideal choice to edit the volumes and he did that with a remarkable talent up to his passing in 1999.

At the last Bologna–Claremont Conference, we inaugurated the Randall Hinshaw Memorial Lecture. This year's conference topic is very appropriate; it is "The euro, the dollar and the future of the international monetary system." The euro, of course, hardly needs any introduction. However, if we think of key things that are going on in the world economy today, a list of subjects of interest would include: the new economy, globalization, the US economic growth rate and record, the [corporate] merger mania that's going on around the world, and the euro. The advent of the euro is certainly going to be an event that will change the character of the international monetary system. It instantly created the second most important currency in the world when it was inaugurated on January 1, 1999. We may as well say that it has created three islands of stability in the world: the euro area, the dollar area, and the yen area. In the 1970s, and even the 1980s, countries had not yet found the right policy mix to combat inflation. The story of the 1990s is that inflation has to a large extent been toned down and each of those three zones of monetary stability had inflation rates consistently less than 3 percent for something like five years. This is very important, because if you add up the GDP of those three zones, you get roughly 60 percent of world GDP.

A big issue that fits into the basic theme of our meeting is that while we have three zones of stability, we have a lot of exchange rate volatility between those three zones. For example, Norway is illustrative of a country that's on the outside of the euro area, but has a great problem whenever the dollar–euro rate changes very much. Therefore, dollar–euro fluctuations are costly to countries outside this area. I think this example gives focus to the paradox, that we have three zones of monetary stability, but we have potentially large fluctuations in exchange rates among these areas, and the question remains as to the risks exchange rate fluctuations impose on the long-run stability of the international monetary system.

It should be noted that the program is not written in stone, it's typed on ordinary paper and we can rip it up and change it as we see fit. A tradition of the Bologna Center series, from the very beginning, has been to go around the table and ask for comments on key elements or observations that people have about the world economy, not necessarily addressing any particular topic, but just what do you think we really need to talk about? Max Cordon, who is going to chair the rest of the morning session, is going to note key elements, and we will try to make any corrections or improvements to the program. We're going to go around the table and have each participant state the key elements that they think we should focus on. I think I'll ask Paul Volcker, since he's the last [to arrive] he'll be punished by being the first.

PAUL VOLCKER: I was almost ready to volunteer, because I can be very brief. I don't know what you started with, but you concluded on what I think the theme of our discussion ought to be. What impressed me in this recent financial crisis in the so-called emerging economies was the level of complications created by the extreme fluctuations in the yen–dollar exchange rate, which, as a matter of fact, were far greater than the recent fluctuations in the euro–dollar exchange rate. I think it is very hard to run a sensible monetary policy, exchange rate policy, or even economic policy in a country when its trade is well diversified between Japan, the United States and Europe, and the currency is fluctuating literally 60–70 percent at times over a year or two. So that brings up the question as to what their exchange rate policy should be. It is difficult to say when the big countries' currencies are so volatile. So you come to the rather basic question of what you can do to stabilize the rates between the so-called zones of stability that you have mentioned. It is a challenge that nobody much wants to talk about. Certainly government officials don't want to talk about it, certainly financial market people that tend to profit from the volatility don't want to talk about it, but we have an opportunity to talk about it here.

ROBERT SKIDELSKY: Well, I did not expect this honor, but I just want to say a couple of things. The first is that this is globalization's second time around. We had a world economy at the end of the 19th century and when you look at what people were predicting for the twentieth century in about 1900, you find that everyone was very optimistic. They believed we were entering into an era of peace and unimaginable prosperity in which trade would bind the nations of the world together. Then the First World War broke out 14 years after that. It seems to me that the central question is how we can do better this time around, and in that respect, how we work out our monetary arrangements will play an important part in the answer to this question because excessive volatility encourages all the forces of economic nationalism, which sour political relations. We have a great challenge in both working out a monetary system that harmonizes the interests of nations and also a trading system that does so as well. I think that this is one of the great challenges.

ARMAND CLESSE: One aspect I think that might be discussed is the perceived or real European deficiencies and/or weaknesses, when it comes to the relationship between the euro and the dollar. For example, the political arrangements underlying the European integration endeavors may affect the so-called weakness of the dollar; what can and should be done about this so we reach a more satisfactory relationship between these two currencies? This is just one aspect that is perhaps not so often discussed at these kinds of meetings.

ROBERT MUNDELL: I just want to mention that in December 1998, Armand held a conference in Luxemburg on a similar topic and the book covering its proceedings has just come out. He has brought with him a few copies for the participants that we will distribute later on. It is entitled *The Euro As a Stabilizer in the International Economic System* (Robert Mundell and Armand Cleese (eds) (2000), Kluwer Academic Publishers); interesting material.

NICOLAS KRUL: One of the things that have struck me in the last few years is that the determinants of exchange rate fluctuations have changed so much. When the euro was conceived we talked about international monetary relations 10 or 15 years ago. We talked about it in terms of the classic adjustment mechanisms, but what has happened in the last few years? Globalization of the international financial system and its enormous growth has brought about a very important change in capital flows, which are now entirely different from what we used to know. This has been accompanied by changes in the financial structure, which are very important. Financial innovation, for instance, has greatly enlarged the capital deployed, but it has at the same time reduced the capital at risk and that is a situation, which, in the case of miscalculations like the Long-Term Capital Management situation, breaks the balance and makes for extraordinary volatility in various markets. Then there is a very important change in risk premium thinking in the financial markets, which has an impact on flows. We used to think in terms of hindsight bias by having notions like mean reversion, but that has more less been thrown out the window, and what we have now is a sort of scenario thinking, which is much more subjective, much more volatile, very much linked to financial expectations which are highly unstable. It is a mistake really to pull the rug out from under the consensus evaluations – what we used to have in the financial markets. And it's not only that this makes for intrinsically greater instability, highly volatile capital flows, but they also have a another aspect which I didn't see very much discussed in the literature and that is that the volatility and instability in the markets gives a premium to the markets which are deeper and more liquid and more predictable than others. I think that one of the reasons why the US dollar has been so different from the initial calculations we did in the euro area is that the American market is by far the most liquid, the most predictable, and the least costly market to operate in. I think that is one of the aspects we should discuss; it is a very important new element in the determination of exchange rates.

VÁCLAV KLAUS: There are many topics that I think we could start with on the list, but I would like to stress one dimension I wish to add to the topics suggested. For many of us, the main interest is to study and to understand the impact of the existing international economic trade, financial, and monetary arrangements on emerging markets both in the developing world and in the post-communist world. This is definitely for us personally, but I think also for the rest of the world, a very interesting issue because we entered the international community suddenly overnight. All the while the world has been dramatically changing. We studied textbooks that were outdated and ill-suited to provide instruction in this new environment. Some important issues I would like to discuss are: what kinds of monetary policies, and what kind of institutional arrangements to introduce as a result of what I would call the enormous fragility and vulnerability of the emerging countries. This vulnerability and fragility was not due to any policy mistake of those countries, but is an unavoidable evolutionary stage of development. What I call fragility and vulnerability can be translated into the notion of deep and shallow markets, these are the terms I sometimes use, and as it is described, the deep markets in the United States are the least costly to operate in. It is quite clear that emerging markets are very shallow. This shallowness means that transactions may be costly and the volatility enormous. It is important to discuss how these issues are understood in international financial institutions, the International Monetary Fund [IMF] and elsewhere. Shallow markets are occasionally dismissed as a policy mistake of one government or another, whereas it may be an unavoidable evolutionary stage. This does not mean we do not make mistakes, we do. However, the costliness between deep and shallow markets is an important part of the whole story.

CHRISTOPHER JOHNSON: My comment contains some good news and some bad news. The good news is that the euro has been a great success internally in Europe. The bad news is that it's been a failure internationally. First, the primary success of the euro: it has removed exchange rate risk among 11 major countries in Europe. This is a precondition of having proper European integrated capital markets. It's already been happening spectacularly in the bond markets; the equity markets will take another five years. As such, an integrated European equity market has yet to materialize. But, nevertheless, the encouragement of trade and economic growth is very considerable. Bob Mundell mentioned the problems of Norway as being an "out" country. I might, being British, mention the problems of the UK. One can describe the withdrawal of BMW from the British motor industry of being at least in part caused by the unforeseen strength of the pound against the euro. This encapsulates the big problems for our manufacturing sector, which is so dependent on trade with Europe. In actuality, there is a trade-off with the exchange rate stability that we have gained in Europe: you get more exchange rate stability within the area but you still have to live with instability outside the area, notably against the dollar and, of course, the yen. But this has always been a feature of the European economy. In fact, if you look at the predecessor currencies of the euro, they were far weaker in 1985, when we had a very strong dollar, than the euro has been in the last year. So, I would say there has not been a notable increase in external instability, but a notable increase in internal stability. Now the bad news: the euro is widely regarded by people inside and outside euro-land as being a failure because of its weakness against the dollar. Now these newspaper readers have not, of course, read any economics. They do not realize what wonderful news it is that Europe has become so much more competitive in terms of its exports into the US and elsewhere, and I think we have to discuss the reasons for this.

To begin with I would attribute the dollar's strength mainly to the amazing strength of the US economy, followed by the strength of Wall Street and the enormous attraction of American equities, which represent a much larger share of American corporate finance than equities do in Europe. America has become a magnet for equity capital, and the outflow of capital from Europe has been much greater than the modest balance of payments surplus that the euro-land countries enjoy. So the net result: A much bigger capital account deficit and therefore a current account surplus leading to a weakening of the currency.

So far this situation has not been as unstable as people predicted. Everybody's been predicting that the thing must turn around, but it is right to go on investing in Wall Street, if you look at today's returns. One can ultimately see Wall Street turning around, the dollar falling, American strengthening its current account by becoming more competitive, and importing less capital. However, Europe has to become better at attracting global capital flows, and in particular, equity flows. There is a great urgency to integrate the European capital markets. Existing national leaders in Europe are running around like headless chickens trying to get together and not usually knowing which direction to move in. Europe has got a lot to do both to reform its labor markets, and its economies, to get economic growth moving, which is just beginning modestly, but also to back this up by attracting capital from the rest of the world and thus ending the enormous asymmetry which must strike us all as we look across the Atlantic.

RICHARD BLACKHURST: I have one small suggestion, something that might be worth a few minutes of our time, and that's the recent report by the Meltzer Commission [chaired by Carnegie Mellon professor Allan Meltzer], the group of 11 American scholars who studied the IMF and World Bank and about two weeks ago issued a report with some recommendations for changing the way the IMF and the World

Bank operate. They were very interesting suggestions. I think they have implications for some of the topics that are on the agenda.

There also is an interesting line of work getting started now in the trade area, but I assume also in the monetary arena as well. It begins with [Washington University economist and 1994 Nobel Laureate] Douglass North's work on the importance of institutions to economic development at the national and sub-national level. As the world integrates, as globalization progresses, many of the findings of Douglass North about the importance of institutional development on a national level are becoming increasingly important at the multilateral level. This gives an intellectual foundation to look at the multilateral institutional requirements as globalization progresses, and you can see the recent Meltzer Commission report as an input into that process as far as the Bank and the Fund are concerned.

MATE BABIC: The introduction of the euro on the first of January 1999 was not necessarily a good thing for countries in transition. Since most of them are export-dependent on the euro area countries, the depreciation of the euro vis-à-vis the United States dollar had deleterious effects on these developing economies. Some of them are heavily indebted countries. Most of their international debts are in dollars; and most of their exports go to the European Union. Due to this high-level of dollar-denominated debt, any rise in the exchange rate of the dollar vis-à-vis the euro hurts the development effort of these countries. For example, what if the interest rates on the international market go up? Since most of these debts were contracted with fluctuating interest rates, any increase in rates will also increase the debt burden for these countries. In addition, a rise in the price of oil could trigger cost inflation and that may recreate the problems that we experienced in the beginning of the 1980s. These countries need capital for their development, but more often than not, they have difficulties paying their existing debts. These developing countries' credibility and their credit ratings are going down. They will likely face very restrictive conditions in the capital market and their development could be put in jeopardy.

GIORGIO BASEVI: I would like to underline some of the suggestions that have already been made. One is concerning the different depths and liquidity of financial markets. Mate [Babic] just stressed that Croatia and other economies in transition have a strange asymmetry between their orientation in terms of trade and their denomination of debt: the dollar being the main currency of denomination of Croatian debt and Croatia exporting most of its trade to the euro-land countries. Why is there such an asymmetry? I think this goes back to the question of market liquidity – the dollar market being the largest in the world.

I would add to this another aspect: the more general question of whether there is a tendency towards reducing the number of currencies relative to the number of countries. This brings in another issue: what about the traditional national roles of regulation, surveillance, and lender of last resort? Will the main monetary authorities also have to take on these roles for the countries and currencies that are tied to them?

Finally, I think we can connect these issues through the problems and the implications of the reduction in government debt that is taking place in most major countries, at least relative to GDP, if not in absolute terms like in the US and the UK. The problem of using national, common, and/or the public debt, is usually analysed from the point of view of how best to use the resources: one either cuts taxes or increase expenditures, and if one increases expenditures, how to invest them as a result of this choice. As such, there are interesting implications for financial markets. In a world where the share of risk-free bonds decreases, financial markets may find themselves a bit more risky. In a way, government debt, at least viable government debt, is a required element in the harmonic structure of financial markets and if the share of, say, the US government debt or the European government debt as a whole were substantially decreased I think there would be important implications for financial markets and I suggest this would be something to analyse.

ROBERT MUNDELL: I wonder, Giorgio; do you think we should approach that subject through the issue of generational accounting?[1]

GIORGIO BASEVI: Yes, it is expensive.

ROBERT MUNDELL: The fact that when we look at budget deficits and public debt we don't take into account expected future liabilities of governments for pension plans so forth is what generational accounting captures. This could be discussed today.

1. See Auerbach, Alan J., Laurence J. Kotlikoff, and Willi Leibfritz, *Generational Accounting Around the World*, Chicago: University of Chicago Press, 1999.

OTMAR ISSING: Our chairman, at the beginning of his introductory statement, referred to three zones of monetary stability, as he called it, in the world. And in that respect, the introduction of the euro indeed has not only changed the face of Europe, but has also had global implications. We now have the second largest economic area in the world, a single currency for almost 300 million people, and an economic area with characteristics in some respects, unfortunately only in some respects, very similar to the United States. EU countries are somewhat more open than any individual country was before the creation of the monetary union. This has important implications. One of which is that this area and participating countries are much less exposed to external shocks than before. And what's going on in the euro area has greater implications for the rest of the world than before.

We therefore move to the question as to the correct policy choices for the euro area. I think on the macroeconomic level, for the time being, the start in almost every respect has been much better than some feared. I think this goes without saying on the monetary policy level, but I would say that even on fiscal policies, the Stability Pact worked better than, I must confess, I personally had expected. After a long period of fiscal consolidation, it had to be expected that efforts to continue would somewhat weaken. And of course in every second monthly bulletin, we admonished governments to do more. But compared to expectations, I think it is going in the right direction and this is good news.

On monetary policy, we have started in an environment of price stability and this is, of course, due to the policies of the national central banks. But now after 15 months, it is more and more the responsibility of the ECB [European Central Bank] and it is our responsibility, which is governed by the expectations of markets. Inflation expectations are very much contained. Markets have given us credibility and we have shown that this situation of price stability is not just an episode, but should be a period of continuous stability.

The euro area continues to experience problems at the micro level. A monetary union needs micro-flexibility, and this is an important contribution to the soundness of the global economy. The euro area is still an economy with much too little flexibility in labor markets – it's highly, highly regulated and experience shows that if deregulation is managed it works. This occurs to the surprise of politicians, but not to economists, because they have always predicted if one deregulates one will see lower prices and stronger economic activity. So reforms can be done, even on the continent. This experience, I think, should now spread and should encourage politicians to move forward with the needed reforms. This is also very important because the success of any monetary union depends, of course, on monetary policy, but to make a single monetary policy for such a diverse and huge economic area successful, we need more micro-flexibility. This is extremely important. The Maastricht Treaty has made a very clear assignment for monetary policy. It has given the European Central Bank a clear mandate to maintain price stability and I think by doing so, by delivering what politicians have promised, namely a stable euro, then we make our best possible contribution to the global economy.

MAX CORDEN: There are already so many topics, I think I'd be making a great contribution by not adding any more. Let me just raise one issue that I think is important. I had a long conversation recently in Japan. Apparently policy in Japan has been unable to remedy their recession. Ideally we should discuss why that is so in Japan and does their experience produce any lessons for Europe and the United States? Could Europe or the United States ever find themselves in that kind of position, where the old-fashioned Keynesian methods don't work and result in a major prolonged recession? That's an issue certainly on my mind.

ENZO GRILLI: I would like to return to and emphasize one topic that has been raised before, albeit from a different angle: the importance of dealing with emerging market economies. The key lessons of the recent crises – the Asia, Brazil, and Russia crises – have been that greater exchange rate flexibility is advisable in many situations. However, these crises affected only emerging market countries. Therefore in the creation of areas of monetary stability, as you call them, does it have consequences for emerging countries, and particularly for their exchange rate policy choices? Are we enlarging or restricting these choices? Are we forcing emerging countries to go towards indirect flexibility by creating areas of monetary stability? Are these choices in the interest, in terms of macro-stability and growth, of these countries? I think when we talk about the international monetary system we have to focus a little bit more on the rest of the membership.

MARIO BALDASSARRI: I do believe the euro depends on Europe, and the dollar depends on the United States. We could give another title to the conference, namely: "Europe, the United States and the International Economic System." Let me start from what Bob Mundell called the paradox: three big areas of monetary stability, a lot of volatility between the three areas and the effect on the rest of the world. I would like to raise three problems: the first one is outside the three areas – what's going on in the rest of the world; the second is inside the three areas; and the third is inside Europe.

First point: Bob said the three big areas represent altogether 60 percent of world GDP, which means that the rest of the world represents 40 percent of GDP. Now, should we take these numbers as fixed for the next few decades and consider our growth in the sense of the three big areas as independent from the rest of the world, or rather is it dependent on the growth of that 40 percent? As such, what are the economic implications? Should we move in the direction of thinking that each of the three areas will assume some kind of tutorship with its neighbors? I mean, should we go towards a system in which North America takes care of South America; Europe will take care of Africa and Eastern Europe; and Japan will take care of Asia? Is it a real international monetary system in which new areas will come into the club? Let's have a look inside the three areas.

The next point I wish to raise here is that I deeply believe that the weakness or strength of a currency is dependent on the economic performance of the system as a whole. But, the performance of the system within each area is clearly dependent on market structures and institutions. If we do believe this, it's clearly the case that the market structures and institutions of the United States won the race with respect to the European and Japanese models. And if we believe this, then Europe and Japan must make the necessary structural reforms – try to accomplish this in some way, within their own original history and tradition, but the target is clearly there.

The United States structure is flexible. But on the other side we have weakness in this reasoning. The first weakness is current account deficit. The strongest economy with the strongest currency has inflows of capital. How far can this go? The second weakness is the stock market bubble. It is quite clear that the good economic performance of the US economy depends on the working of the bubble, at least in the last two or three years. Finally, inside Europe, it's quite clear that we cannot go much further having a single currency and 11 budgets. So the point is, if we do not wish to go back to 11 currencies, and we wish to have for the next few decades one currency, how can we manage eleven budgets? And I wish to raise the question of competition or coordination.

ROBERT BARTLEY:　I notice that on the program we have an item – the euro and monetary discipline. Now monetary discipline is the easy part. At the risk of taking a leap I'd suggest that the success of the euro, in terms of reinvigorating the European economies, depends on its effect as a fiscal discipline. Obviously the inability of national central banks to monetize government debt is an enormously important development with the euro. The question is how this discipline will work itself out. Will it take the kind of narrow-minded view present in the Maastricht criteria that the only thing that counts is a reduction of government debt, because that makes the problem of the central bank easier? Or, will it lead within Europe to a competition for the most effective fiscal policies, which I suspect would be returning some of these flows to the private sector and reducing the overhead of the public sector, which I think is obviously too large in most European countries. For example, will the rest of Europe succeed in forcing Ireland to harmonize its tax policies upward, or will Germany and France find it necessary to start reducing their tax rates and their public sector in order to compete with the Celtic tiger? I think right at the moment that is the key issue on the agenda, although admittedly it takes us somewhat astray from the issue of monetary policy.

ROBERT PRINGLE:　I am especially interested in the challenges facing central bankers referred to already by many speakers around the table. The last quarter of the twentieth century saw a really remarkable shift towards the independence of central banks. Governments let central banks basically run a very large part of economic policy [monetary policy], in a remarkable historical experiment. They are still working out the implications of that independence. I am particularly interested in questions of institutional design and the institutional details of central banks. Most governments have reformed the legislation governing central banks in recent years. The questions of how they are governed, the question of independence, the questions of transparency and accountability – not just in the European Central Bank context, but in most other of the 173 central banks around the world, are important.

There are numerous macroeconomic challenges facing central banks. There is the whole question of the new economy, and do these developments imply that the economy is going to be run at a lower level of unemployment permanently than had been the case before. Many speakers have already referred to the challenge facing central banks dealing with asset price bubbles. Then there is the terrible example of Japan, which is frightening many central banks around the world. There is the whole question of dollarization. It is not good news for my magazine [*Central Banking*] because it might mean fewer numbers of customers as the number of central banks decline. Also, I noticed that Paul Volcker was recently advocating one currency for the world, which would not be good news for my magazine as well. The question of reserve management issues facing central banks is important, especially outside Europe, with the change in the whole reserve base of the system with the coming of the euro. How do non-European, and non-US central banks manage their external reserves of gold and foreign currencies? Then there is the question of risk management for central banks themselves. Central banks often recommend better risk management practices to commercial banks, but have yet to address risk management practices in their own organizations. Also we should discuss the question of the central bank's relationship with governments in the future. As I said, central banks have been given a remarkable degree of independence, not just in getting to a particular level of inflation, but sometimes they are able to set their own inflation goals. How long will the political realm continue to give central banks that remarkable degree of independence? The question of the relationship between central banking and political authorities I think will be very important for the future design of the world economy.

EMIL CLAASSEN: I'm looking at the triangle of the US dollar, yen and euro. This system works perfectly well; it's a floating exchange rate system. In addition, the United States is traditionally neutral with respect to the exchange rate to the euro and the yen. Now that is for me a puzzle. Certainly the inflation rate experiences are compatible and extremely low.

In my modeling, the world interest rate is the United States interest rate because the world uses the US dollar. So that may be one issue: Should we define the world interest rate in terms of the American interest rate [after the introduction of the euro]?

HERBERT GIERSCH: I would like to look at the relationship between real exchange rates and real economic growth, particularly with reference to the euro–dollar real rate, which is the basis for forming a judgment as to whether the euro, at the present stage, is over- or undervalued. There may be short-run, medium-run and long-run aspects which contribute to our judgments in this respect. The questions are where do we produce, what do we produce, and how do the terms of trade factor into our decision. The question then arises, what is the implicit exchange rate between different locations? This is a general question with regard to the notion of where to find the real exchange rate – should it be fixed or rather determined between the euro and the dollar? There are many locational factors that play a role in the long run, in the medium run and in the short run.

In the long run, one must focus on location with regard to the center. Here I must say that the United States, or dollar-land, is the center of the world economy, which implies that it eventually should have one currency. But then the question arises, what are the expensive and cheap places in such a system? The most expensive place is generally the center. If then the United States turns out to be the center of the world economy, then the dollar should be relatively more expensive, which should be make the US a relatively more expensive place in the world, and every so-called "catching-up" country, or "catching-up" location, should become more expensive in terms of the implicit real exchange rate, which I would look to in order to form a judgment of whether the euro is overvalued or is undervalued.

At this point I have to say that medium-term factors play an important role in forming this judgment. Namely, the resource flows that take place from countries like euro-land towards dollar-land, which means the dollar-land is growing faster than Europe, and therefore has a current account deficit. My way of thinking stresses resource flows and considers them important. I would expect trade to adjust to [the exchange rate], i.e. that there is more sustainability in the current account deficits if they are financed by real flows of capital from peripheral areas to the center. But then the question arises in the medium term, why does this capital, if it is so important in forming a judgment about the real exchange rate, why is this capital moving towards the United States? In contrast to my prejudice that rich countries should export capital to the developing countries, I pose the following question: if capital flows are the dominant force in the picture, can we conclude that the current account deficit of the United States is sustainable because it is freely financed by capital moving towards the center? We arrive at my central question: why does

Europe export capital that it could well use given the other resources available in euro-land? The answer to this question involves the notion of deregulation and flexibility.

Most of you are aware that there is an index of economic freedom that relates economic growth and institutional freedom. There is a lot of research that indicates that the freer the country is with regards to investment and other economic activities, the higher is the real growth rate; therefore, we have a factor determining capital flows from the less liberalized countries of Europe to the more liberalized United States. There are other factors involved since this is a new economy. I conjecture that the center is using its advantages of agglomeration, but it is also producing new knowledge. Then the question arises: how can Europe, given that it would like to improve its real exchange rate vis-à-vis the dollar, catch up to the US with regard to economic freedom and production of knowledge? So my principal question is about real exchange rates and economic growth: What is the relationship between euro-land and dollar-land, and can we form a judgment about whether the euro at the present stage is overvalued or undervalued?

ROBERT MUNDELL: What a fascinating catalogue of things to discuss. The idea of the center from location theory is an interesting one. It's not completely unconnected to Emil Claassen's argument of what the real interest rate is.

ALEXANDRE LAMFALUSSY: My query is based on the observation that the financial systems of the developed world, under the guidance of what is happening in the United States in particular, are evolving at an accelerated pace towards a market-centric system, as opposed to the old bank-dominated, or bank-centric system. Now that has really transformed the financial scene in the United States, but it is beginning to affect Europe as well at a rate that people do not fully realize. What are the implications of this?

I think most of us would probably agree that this is going to be a more efficient system, both in the technical sense used by economists, and also in a common sense use of the term, i.e. it would lead to a more efficient allocation of resources. But will it lead to less instability in financial markets? I was tending to believe that it would lead to less instability until I saw what happened in the United States, not so much in the equity markets, which was not new, but in the US government debt market in September and October 1998. I do not refer simply to the Long-Term Capital Management [LTCM] experience, which in itself was quite frightening, but something else happened in that market, it was not simply a flight into quality [a highly leveraged liquidity crisis]; it was a flight into liquidity. Also recall that during that time the Fed cut its rates twice and Wall Street responded. But by the time Wall Street reached its pre-crisis level, there was still what the Fed said in its communiqué: the unusual strains in the US debt and credit markets that prompted a third decrease in the interest rate. That was basically due to the considerable liquidity risk premium in the Treasury bond market. How is it that the most transparent, most liquid, and deepest financial market in the world got into such trouble?

Financial asset prices in a nation are based on two things: leverage and liquidity or lack thereof. What governs movements towards liquidity? And what happens in a system where even large interest rate or asset price changes do not clear the market? These are very serious problems, and again I don't want to say that the direction in which we are going is a bad one, because I am basically convinced that in terms of efficiency it will be far better than anything the old style banking system has ever produced. But I'm not sure that it does not raise other questions about instability.

AXEL LEIJONHUFVUD: One concern of mine is that I think much of our thinking about policy is based on short memories. Bob Mundell started by talking about the three areas of stability and almost all of us have referred to it since. What he said was that they had stability in the sense of lower inflation for five years or more. Well it seems to me that much of our current discussion is still dominated by the policies that were required to beat inflation, which is basically that of fiscal reform, of creating sustainable government financial situations. For example consider the criticism of the IMF over Indonesia. The IMF stepped in and obviously was thinking of Indonesia as another example of a Latin American country of ten years before. Their thinking was completely dominated by models of how you stabilize Argentina or Brazil. It seems to me that the current fashion for inflation targeting as the central bank policy of choice, and for that matter the independence of central banks, is also dominated by the memories of previous inflations.

In a world where governments respect their intertemporal budget constraints, monetary policy can have significant effects on real rates and on the real liquidity of markets and therefore on asset prices, investment, and growth in ways that they cannot have in settings where because of unsustainable fiscal policy, the central banks are trying to combat the inflationary pressures arising from government budgetary problems. Now, why do I bring this up? Well, we have been talking about the instability of the exchange rates in the triangle and it seems to me that the history of the yen to dollar rate in the last ten years is altogether a story of the aftermath of the Japanese bubble. And the Japanese bubble developed without any inflation. The Japanese Central Bank in the 1980s could just as well have been running an inflation target regime and it wouldn't have made any difference. The question now is whether the euro to dollar rate is not dominated by what in effect is an American bubble. You will remember that Keynes always dealt with share prices as determined by what he called the balance between bulls and bears. But in the US, the last bear has been dead and gone for a couple of years now. There are only the bulls left. No bearish fund manager could keep his job. So is the US situation sustainable? Well I share the skepticism that Lamfalussy just voiced. So what is the point? I think that just keeping inflation low in these three areas separately, will not suffice to keep capital flows at manageable levels, or to stabilize exchange rates and therefore, I think we have to rethink some old lessons about macroeconomic policies.

MANFRED NEUMANN: We have heard many issues this morning, and I want to add the following. The euro is not just a new currency; it is a currency that will grow. We have not seen that it will grow due to more international demand for it, which, if we had observed this phenomenon would imply that this currency would turn into an international currency. The question is whether and for what time this currency will be a large local currency. This is presently an open question.

From where does the growth potential of the euro come? It comes from the fact that governments have an interest in joining the euro area. This has implications for monetary policy, but also for exchange rate policy. Also the question of who in the euro area has the authority to conduct international negotiations on, say, exchange rate behavior, or interventions is open. The enlargement over the next ten to 15 years will strengthen the ECB's ability to run monetary policy, though it will become more difficult to have a consensus on policy if institutional reforms fail to be implemented. As you know, in the ECB, policy decisions are completed through a sort of consensus – there is no voting. This setup might make it difficult as more countries are admitted into the organization. All of this means that there will likely be more delay and the organization will be more passive instead of active when the latter may be necessary.

On the other hand, a similar problem should arise at the European Council, which is the Council of the Economic and Finance Ministers. This European Council is where the general exchange rate policy declarations are made. The more people there, the less likely it will be that they will ever issue declarations. This is good news for the ECB. It is difficult to say how all of this will unfold, but clearly, the ECB will have to think about their long-run exchange rate policy. At present, I do not know what their exchange rate policy is. They might have the attitude of being inward looking; that is, concentrating on the internal stability of the currency. And we do know that by means of monetary policy you affect the course of the exchange rate. On the other hand, if you want your currency to become an international currency, then you would have to look at the fact that some countries might simply decide to replace their national currency by the euro without being members of the European Union, similar to South American countries replacing their national currency by the dollar. The question is what effects does this have on the Fed, or say on the US on the one hand, and on the euro area on the other hand?

ANDRÉ SZASZ: I would like to limit myself to one topic if I may, and that is the question alluded to by others and also quite relevant to the issues that Alexandre Lamfalussy discussed and that is, what are the prospects in the longer run for the euro area to contribute to global economic stability? It seems to me that that depends first of all on the question of how inward looking the area will turn out to be in the years to come. Additionally, one must ask on what this depends.

First of all, this will depend on the degree of homogeneity of its countries. After the process of widening, which is going to continue and which is not so easy to say in advance how far it will go, what seems to be very likely is that in the course of that process, euro-land is going to become even less homogeneous than it is now. Interests will not always be the same and that is a force that may induce a tendency towards inward looking.

Secondly, we have the question of policy. Mr. Issing pointed out that as far as the stability pact is concerned, it could be worse. No doubt it could be. We have been fortunate in the sense that the cyclical situation helped here and there, but we must further ask: what about structural development?

Thirdly, what is the timetable for structural reforms, which all governments say are necessary? To put it differently, there is no doubt that we have a monetary union, but I am not sure as to the extent of our economic union. Recall that there was a time when many of us were convinced that one was not possible without the other.

NIELS THYGESEN: I would like to come back to the question of exchange rate instability. I think as economists we have a major problem at the present time in explaining why the euro has become as weak as it has. Some turn to the long-run structure explanations like Herbert Giersch. I am surprised, though, that he is still in doubt whether the euro is over or undervalued.

If we look at traditional economic measures, fundamental equilibrium exchange rate calculations or other methods of long-run equilibrium, they all seem to suggest that the euro is currently undervalued, in fact quite substantially. But if we look at the shorter-term cyclical factors that could explain why the euro is currently weak, they all seem to have deficiencies and we obviously do not understand it. Some said in 1999 that it is due to the unexpectedly strong growth in the United States. But this strengthening of the dollar vis-à-vis the euro has continued in the second half of the year up to the present (although there is now a recovery in Europe and interest rate differentials have in fact narrowed between the US and Europe). Additionally, some have said it is the boom in the US market, which makes for massive shifts of capital out of Europe. In fact however, there seems to be little correlation between the US share price indices and the exchange rate. So again here we have a problem.

Some have said it is because borrowers have found it very attractive, earlier than investors, to use issues of euro-denominated bonds. This is largely by people inside the euro area and should not have implications for the exchange rate. So, in the absence of good short-run explanations and the vague nature of the longer-run structural phenomenon, I fear that the public debate has centered on whether the explanation can be found in some bungling by the European Central Bank.

I do not think that this is a viable explanation. It can maybe explain a little bit, but it cannot be the major factor. I think it's one that we should not overlook and we will probably come to when we discuss the formulation of targets for monetary policy in the United States and in Europe in a comparative perspective.

PAUL ZAK: I want to mention something discussed by Mr. Klaus and Professor Grilli regarding development. It seems clear that at least two areas of the three mentioned by Bob Mundell have a comparative advantage of producing monetary stability: the US and the EU. If that is the case, then why do we not see more countries adopting one of these two stable currencies? For example, this month the president of Ecuador advocated dropping their local currency and using the US dollar. Within a week he was pushed out of office; this was not a stable outcome from his countrymen's point of view, which seems very strange. I think if we're moving towards a global situation with a few currency areas, we have to ask, why is the rate of adoption so slow? What are the barriers to adoption? And what are the benefits of the reduced volatility relative to the loss of flexibility?

MAX CORDEN: Let us now move our discussion to fiscal policy, labor markets and exchange rates.

VÁCLAV KLAUS: The politicians are definitely less academic than the rest of the group, so I should not start. Nevertheless, I would like to make two comments about the internal aspects of the euro. Professor Issing mentioned that the euro was probably the greatest change in central banking. I would definitely say that it was the greatest voluntary shift of sovereignty in history. This is, in my opinion, a crucial part of the whole process and a serious question would be, who did it voluntarily? I think that probably the European politicians did it. And I am afraid that the European citizens did not do it either voluntarily or even intentionally, and I have the feeling that they were not aware of what has been really done, what has been really achieved.

I do not believe in the possibility of having such an asymmetric arrangement – having monetary union without fiscal union and without political union – and to illustrate I always turn to my personal experience. I used to be the minister of finance of a dissolving monetary union called Czechoslovakia and as I tried to keep the country together, I really understood that you cannot have one [monetary union] without the other [fiscal union]. Our ambition was, even after liquidating the political union and the fiscal union, to keep the monetary union going.

So I have some personal experience in this respect and for me this is the real issue.

It seems to me those countries – small, open economies – next to euro-land soon will be in a position similar to Austria on the one hand and the Netherlands [during the 1980s and 1990s] on the other. They would belong to what used to be something like the German currency zone without being a formal member of that zone. I can very easily imagine that the small Central European countries will be, relatively soon after entering the EU, able to enter the European Monetary Union as well.

MARIO BALDASSARRI: Let me start with a question and an answer. The question is, will the euro make a stronger Europe, or will a growing Europe make a stronger euro? As I understand it, we agree that a growing Europe can make a stronger euro. If this is the answer, I wish to put a question on the table. We have spoken about microeconomics, and we are planning to have a deeper discussion on these topics – market flexibility, institutions and so on. The point I wish to raise, which is an important macro point, is the following: there is a real confusion in Europe between financial intermediation by the state and real intermediation by the state. What we had in the Maastricht Treaty, within the Stability Pact, is a target that attempts to achieve zero state financial intermediation in the future, i.e. the zero deficit/GDP ratio. But we have yet to discuss it, and I think that we should now discuss this point about the state's real intermediation, where for example in Europe, the state intermediates roughly 50 percent of GDP in terms of government expenditure and tax revenue. I do believe that a zero deficit/GDP ratio coming from 50 percent of government expenditure, is not the same as a zero deficit/GDP ratio coming from 90 percent of government expenditure or 20 percent of government expenditure.

If I go far back 25 years when MIT economist and 1987 Nobel Laureate, Bob Solow was teaching growth theory, we have understood since then that there could be differences in countries' growth experiences. I would like to emphasize the following: either the European states can demonstrate through empirical evidence that by intermediating 50 percent of GDP the state is able to have long-run sustainable growth, or we need to move the border between state and market in all European countries. If you look at the figures, at least over the last ten years, it is quite clear that the state, by intermediating 50 percent of GDP, is not able to achieve long-run growth above 3 percent a year. Answering the question is very easy, because it depends on the way in which states allocate resources as compared to the way in which private markets allocate resources.

To sum up, let me restate two short conclusions. I feel we should discuss proposals on how to decrease fiscal pressure in European countries, down at least ten percentage points relative to GDP over the next three to four years. Given that we have to respect the Growth and Stability Pact, what types of government expenditure reforms are available to us?

PAUL VOLCKER: In terms of the sustainability and political acceptability of the euro, I always hear this comment that you do not have fiscal offsets to differential shocks in different countries as compared to the United States – it is always compared to the United States – and I guess I do not understand the argument, because it seems to me with the amount of government expenditures and taxes in Europe, and even if it comes down 10 percent, it is much larger than in the United States. So you will have an automatic cushioning within the constraints of the Stability Pact, which may in fact be a little too strict, but if you met the balanced budget criteria, then you have quite a lot of room for an automatic stabilizer working in different areas within Europe, then national budgets, rather than a European-wide budget, is flexible in this context. But this picture of the United States having this immense fiscal flexibility, although it is true there is an automatic stabilizer from the federal budget, the idea that there is a differential adjustment for different economic impacts in different states is simply not true. The states do not have much and the last time the federal government made any discretionary allocation of budgetary fines or tax reductions to favor individual states is beyond my memory. It just does not happen for political reasons. So you get the automatic effect of a stabilizer, but you get very little, if any, discretionary adjustment. I just do not see why this argument has been so prominent in the European discussion about the sustainability of the euro. There are lots of other areas of concern, the flexibility of the labor market and all the rest, but this particular objection never has seemed to me to be particularly valid and if I am wrong, I would like to hear about it.

Let me make an observation as an observer of a company that has a lot of business in Europe. It does not seem to me that the promise of the euro increasing competition and affecting investment behavior has occurred. There are other factors one has to look at, and it certainly seems to have stimulated a reallocation of investment within Europe, both to make it more efficient within the euro-area, but also to stimulate investment within the euro-area as opposed to the UK, because of the uncertainty of the exchange rate relationship. I would just like to hear more about whether you all agree with this observation.

Finally I want to make another comment about something I have helped stimulate in terms of research. This business about what effect exchange rate instability really has on investment, productivity, efficiency, etc. is obscure, but I have encouraged the Conference Board to undertake a survey among businesses as to what influence exchange rate volatility has on their investment plans. One aspect of this study will cover what is going on within the continent of Europe. I hope that this will be a useful study; they are going to spend a fair amount of money and they have a lot of experience. [Michigan economist] Marina Whitman has agreed to supervise the study, so it has some very responsible academic and economic inputs. I think it will be 18 months from now before we see any results [published report is 'Do exchange rates matter', by Gail D. Foster, The Conference Board Report R-1349-04-RR, 2004]. It is an initiative that interests me because there is so little information on this area other than anecdotal kinds of remarks. We hope to get a little more concrete evidence of something or other. I do not know what it will show, but I think it will be of some interest.

AXEL LEIJONHUFVUD: I would just like to respond very quickly to one of the points raised by Otmar Issing. That is the question of whether the euro itself will act as a sort of catalyst for change and perhaps may end up strengthening the economic leg of the European Monetary Union [EMU], which is one thing that is clearly missing. I think we are going very fast in that direction and I certainly agree with you. The main channel through which the action goes is, of course, the fact that the euro has removed the single most important obstacle to the development of a single market for goods and services. Through transparency, for example, it has a fantastic effect on competition in addition to the effect is has on investment flows and financial restructuring, which in itself produces an effect on national legislations. For example: what happened a few days ago when three of the European stock exchanges decided to merge – Paris, Amsterdam and Brussels? They came up to the very practical problem – where should the headquarters of the company be located? They ended up having to go to Holland, because

Dutch law was the most convenient. That immediately triggered some thinking about the need to have a European-wide company statute, which was more or less buried over the last 20 years. This sort of thing is going to happen, and it brings up the problem of taxation in every possible and conceivable field. The real problem lies in two fields: one is whether the harmonization will happen through market pressures, or through the attempt of governments to try to harmonize. That is one question, and of course I would agree with most of those who say that if the governments have to harmonize, they will harmonize in their own way. There is danger in this. Now the second problem is the constitutional structure of the European Union. We clearly need some sort of effective cooperation between governments. Will that happen in the way that was originally foreseen by the founding fathers through an enlarged power of the commission, or will that happen through intergovernmental cooperation?

PAUL FABRA: I want to make a few quick remarks about the weakness of the euro in the light of the independence of the ECB as enshrined within the treaty as mentioned by Mr. Issing. There are two entities in Europe that are very happy with a weak euro: the socialist German government and the socialist French government. This, it seems to me, is a very important factor. The conventional wisdom would say that the ECB's council, with 11 people having their independent wills, and that independent will should translate into the will of the ECB as such. I challenge very much the idea that the Bundesbank still has an independent will, and the same challenge could be directed to the Bank of France. Therefore, within the treaty as it functions today, I think that the Bundesbank and the Bank of France also have no choice except to interpret the will of the political entities within their borders, namely, the German and French governments and so on.

NIELS THYGESEN: I would like to comment on something Otmar Issing had metioned. It is surprising to see all the criticism of the transparency of the European Central Bank, the way it runs its independence, because if you look at the explanations given by officials of the central bank through the excellent monthly bulletin and the press conferences, they are at least as clear as what you hear from the Federal Reserve Chairman [Alan Greenspan], who is normally praised as the model for transparency. So I think this is a somewhat surprising criticism. It may be due to the difficult transition stage in which the ECB finds itself.

The two-pillar strategy of the bank to use money both as a reference value and a number of other indicators for inflation, does create a bit of confusion in the markets. For example, last spring when the bank lowered the short-rate by half a percent, money growth was far above the reference rate at that time, and that was surprising in a way to markets, although it reassured other critics of the bank, because it showed that the bank was not averse to sustaining the growth potential in Europe at a time when inflationary risks were low. But there may be some technical problems that have to be resolved, particularly since it has not been made clear what the inflationary expectations of the ECB are and the time horizon over which it will try to control inflation. These are important technical issues that may be resolved with time, but they have yet to be resolved at present.

The nature of temporary inflationary shocks, such as the current rise in energy prices, whether that should really lead to any tightening of policy is unclear. If you want only to control the second round effects of such shocks, you need to publish something like a co-inflation rate. And my plea is that the ECB does need to come to terms with the inflation forecast in order to make a better and more predictable impact on markets.

3. Internal aspects of the euro

Introduced by

Robert Bartley

ROBERT BARTLEY: I think it might be a good note to start the afternoon by underlining what Václav Klaus and others said this morning, which is that the introduction of the euro is an absolutely stunning innovation. There is a supranational central bank that is running the euro, and if you stop to think about it, that is something that would have been unthinkable only a few years ago. I do not know if there is any historical example of such a creature, although I suppose if anyone could come up with one it would be Bob [Mundell]. Nevertheless, it is really a stunning development and could be a precedent for an even larger development like a world central bank.

In terms of the internal questions that arise, the first question you have to consider is the temptation that having started this magnificent experiment of a supranational central bank, do you want to build a new nation-state to fit under it? I think this is the wrong way to go. The surrender of sovereignty that was involved in the creation of this new central bank was a very bold step for the European leaders and for [former Chancellor of Germany Helmut] Kohl in particular, however I think the markets also had something to do with it and reduced the sovereignty that nation-states used to have.

The principal use of monetary sovereignty was to inflate nine months before an election. Money illusion would mean that the real effect came before the monetary effect, yet the markets have shortened that period of money illusion time down to something almost non-existent. So governments were giving up a sovereignty they did not really have.

The question of whether to build a nation-state under this new central bank is a question of coordination versus competition – which do you really want? Do you want coordination of fiscal policy or do you want competition in fiscal and regulatory policy? Now if I thought that coordination could bring down the government's share of GDP by ten percentage points in three or four years, I would be for that, but I do not think that that is a likely outcome. I think it is more likely that coordination will lead to, at best, stagnation.

But if the goal is to move to the root of competition among the units underneath this monetary umbrella, a close analogy would be the states in the United States, each of whom has its own budget, but cannot monetize their debt. The result of this has been, in many places, constitutional impediments to issuing debt except through referendum, with repayment schedules and self-financing arrangements. Meanwhile, the states are left to compete so that they all recognize by now that if they increase their taxes it reduces their industrial development, so you have a very healthy kind of competition going on.

We have just gone through an episode in which US states have been frustrated, at least so far, in trying to break out of this discipline by taxing sales over the Internet. This has so far been defeated. So I think the way that Europe ought to develop is to allow some competition so that Holland can become the Delaware of Europe where all the corporations are chartered, where Ireland, while it's very small, can become the tax-incentive capital of Europe. Those things ought to be allowed to flourish and will be much better if one refrains from attempting to build a new nation-state but allow competition among the existing units.

ROBERT SKIDELSKY: I want to address a similar question, which was asked by Dr. Issing, which is whether the euro is bound to lead to political unification. I think for England that is a particularly important question. I hate to introduce Britain's parochial concerns into this global discussion, but in Britain, opinion is pretty clear that if political unification is entailed by membership of the euro, then Britain cannot be part of it. But I would argue first of all that it is not entailed; political unification is not a logical consequence of the formation of the euro. For reasons that Paul Volcker outlined earlier, one can deal with asymmetric shocks through the existing fiscal mechanisms. There is no need to have a central budget for redistributive purposes. So I do not think there is any logical connection between the formation of the euro and European political unification.

On the other hand, there is an independent dynamic towards political unification that still has some way to go. It is not connected logically with the single currency, but it is there. On the other side, though, there is also a very strong dynamic toward central bank independence. And those two things are not easily compatible. So you end up by asking the question: what sort of animal is the European Union now and what will it become in the future? One might think that in historical terms it is a complete chimera; it is something that has not happened before. But I do think there is an historical analogy. Everything in Europe seems to me to have happened before. The analogy I would draw is that of the Holy Roman Empire, which was marked by weak central power – the emperor – and a very strong centralized papacy. The emperor had armies and the pope had theology, anathemas and excommunications. And there was some sort of rough balance of power between these two forces – between the material and the spiritual power. I think something like this is emerging at the moment. In history there is nothing new, it is just the old actors wearing new clothes.

GIORGIO BASEVI: I would also like to link my comments to Otmar Issing's suggestions, and he made at least two. One, what are the implications for institutional arrangements of the creation of the European central banking system, and two, is the euro going to act as a catalyst for further changes? I would take them both together and say something, which adds perhaps to what Alexandre Lamfalussy said before.

As for unifying the market, we tend to think about the labor market but in fact what is going ahead very fast now, as Alexandre [Lamfalussy] mentioned, is the unification of financial markets in Europe. It is not just that the stock exchanges are merging in various ways; it is really that now all the shares and common debts in euro-land are denominated in euros. If you take Italian government debt or French government debt or German government debt, once you have left out the exchange rate risk, and there is very little political risk, there is nothing really different among them. So what is emerging is just one market for government debt. This is a consequence of the euro. It just so happens by historical accident that this unification of denomination in euros happened at about the same time when a tremendous revolution in technology occurred, of course I mean information technology, which is sweeping through financial markets. This is a story that is playing around the world, but it has particularly important implications within Europe. In Europe, the need to restructure the various stock exchanges and markets comes at the same time as this new industrial revolution. So what is happening is that Europe is ahead of the United States, except for Internet businesses, in organizing or reorganizing markets on electronic systems. Now this is just an historical accident, but it's a very important one, because it plays on the question of whether the euro or the liquidity of the markets in euros, will catch up with the liquidity of the market in dollars. So it is both the euro and this strange historical coincidence of the technology revolution that is happening and making market changes.

I come now to institutional changes and I would like to connect them to the euro. This reshuffling, reorganization, and unification of markets in Europe, both driven by the euro and by the new industrial revolution, requires some rethinking of institutions. There have been comments about institutional competition on the tax level or other levels. Here is another level where regulation and surveillance by central banks must, in my view, be centralized. I know that national central banks are very jealous of their independence not in the monetary field, but in the field of regulation and surveillance of their banking systems and markets. But unless you come to some centralization of these roles, businesses will relocate. And so this joint evolution of market integration under the euro denomination, and under the technology revolution, requires in my view a new treaty where the design of the European central banking system is pushed further towards the centralization of regulation and surveillance.

MANFRED NEUMANN: Whether the euro will become a strong currency or not clearly depends on the monetary policy of the ECB, but more so on various real forces and therefore on questions like labor markets. I think the labor markets in Europe are the main matter of concern, because in the large countries like Germany, Italy or France, we still have this inflexible structure due to the fact that we have bargaining at the industry level. In Germany, about 80 percent of the employed people live under contracts that were negotiated by the unions. I think it is similar in Italy and in France and if you do not change this then relative wage levels will be too high, and therefore unemployment will stay high. This I think must be a matter of concern if one looks at the long-run prospects of the euro. I do believe this will change but it is a very gradual process because it can only change by market pressure, which entails companies, one after the other, leaving the employers' associations or workers leaving the unions. We can see this is underway at least in Germany. But it will take another ten to 15 years until politicians feel strong enough to really change the situation. It's written down in the German Constitution that both sides of the labor market, that is employers and employees, can organize to negotiate wages. This is a big problem Europe has to overcome if it wants to compete with the United States.

The other issue is the fiscal question. I am not sure whether I share Otmar Issing's optimism, but we would have to look at the numbers. For example, has Greece really shown such nice fiscal performance so far that they should be admitted [to the European Union]? If Greece joins, then other countries in the future can join with similar performance, which could be a problem. It seems to me that in the [European] Union there is an attitude that says: one small country does not make a difference, but many small countries can make a difference; therefore, one has to be careful.

If we get into bad times, the question of a political union will become very important in terms of the effectiveness of fiscal policy. In good times, the pressures moving us towards political unification are less pronounced. Only a political union can, in bad times, shield the ECB against pressure from politics to adjust their policies to the bad situation in an irresponsible fashion. Here I would like to emphasize that political union does not mean that we need centralization. For example, Germany is a political union, it is a federal union and at this time there's a strong move within Germany to give more of the power back to the so-called lenders, i.e. the German states. So you can have very different types of political unions and it is clear that for Europe I would prefer a political union where the power resides more in the countries and not so much at the center.

To solve the fiscal problem, we do not need as much harmonization as some believe; but there is a problem with the fiscal constraints. One of the problems is that we do not know what the ECB wants to do with respect to stabilization of global shocks. Before the union, each country had a fiscal policy and a monetary policy; they could use both respond to global shocks. We could have a joint policy to combat the effects of these shocks. If the ECB does not take care of these global-type shocks, then countries will have to respond to these shocks at the national level. If you consider the deficit requirement – each country's deficit shouldn't be larger than 3 percent of GDP – then this limits the countries' ability to respond to these shocks.

The second problem in this respect is the following: suppose you want to implement large-scale tax reform, really getting tax rates down. The deficit constraint hinders one's ability to do so because clearly if one does this, immediately the country's fiscal authority will lose the revenue, but the spending remains. So you get then the large deficit, which is not permitted. This fiscal constraint, which we have written into the Maastricht Treaty, now hinders in performing large-scale tax reform. So we have two problems in this respect, but let me add that the advantage of having this deficit constraint helps us to rein in countries that have a history of excessive spending.

RICHARD COOPER: I also want to address some of the questions posed by Otmar Issing. In opening this session, he solicited comments both on the strategy that the ECB has followed so far and on the institutional set up. So I give the remarks of at least one person from the western side of the Atlantic who is sympathetic to the basic enterprise of creating a common currency in Europe and I would say that the strategy has been pretty good. It has not been perfect, but you are just starting out and it is not even clear what perfect means under these circumstances. I think that deciding on a well-defined target, for example monetary targeting, would have been vastly premature. So I think the strategy that was adopted, which has some ambiguities in it to be sure, was in fact the right strategy. Until we all learn how this new enterprise settles down and how the national economies adjust to a common currency, having sharp, well-defined monetary targets would have been a mistake. So I think that the strategy of keeping your eye on movements in the general level of prices and looking at all indicators is basically the right strategy.

I am much less enthusiastic about the present institutional arrangements. They were handed to the ECB by the Maastricht Treaty and the Stability Pact. I said in January 1992, that if Europe takes the Maastricht Treaty seriously, it condemns itself to a decade of stagnation. Europe did take the Maastricht Treaty seriously and sure enough it had a decade of very unimpressive growth. I think it was a direct consequence of the targets set up in the Maastricht Treaty. That is now gone; the cost has already been incurred. I think a common currency was possible without incurring this cost, but that is water over the dam.

The powers that be in Europe decided that the fiscal targets in the Maastricht Treaty should not simply be entry requirements, but rather they should be permanent requirements. Several speakers, including Manfred [Neumann] just now, have spoken to that point. I think that the Growth and Stability Pact, which focuses almost exclusively on stability and says nothing about growth, is simply a mistake. Somehow the Europeans should find their way gracefully to de-commit themselves from the fiscal straightjacket in which they have put themselves. The key feature of the Maastricht Treaty is that national governments should not have access to the central bank in financing their deficits; that is essential, it is in there, but with that feature it is not necessary, in my view, to have further targets on the fiscal side and I think that Europe will come to regret it in times of serious stress. However, there are some "weasel words" in the Stability Pact, which should provide all of the flexibility that is needed.

The other institutional feature that I think is simply unacceptable, is the lack of political accountability of the ECB. This is not an economic point; this is an issue concerning democratic theory. The ECB is not politically accountable to anyone. The Bundesbank was politically accountable. The Federal Reserve is politically accountable, not to the sitting government, but to the governmental and political process. Paul Volcker is here, he can I'm sure affirm this, that the Fed pays very close attention to bills submitted to Congress to change the Federal Reserve Act. Most of them are completely absurd, but nonetheless, they are a source of potential concern. So central bank behavior is constrained, as it should be in a democracy, by public acceptability and that feature is lacking in the current [European] institutional arrangements.

A final point concerns the price target. As I understand it, it is a range, which I think is good, zero to two [percent], measured in terms of a euro-land-wide consumer price index. And that is the point I want to focus on: the consumer price index. There is a growing dissatisfaction in the United States over our consumer price index. We have actually made a number of adjustments in last few years, which have knocked about four-tenths of a percentage point off the growth of the CPI during the 1990s. It is my judgment that the CPI, as measured in the United States, exaggerates the rate of price increases. Agreeing on the amount that it exaggerates is a very difficult technical problem. The fact is we have an upward bias in our units of measurement and that is most dramatic in the area of health care. Any of you who have aging parents, for example, or somebody who is seriously ill in the family, knows what dramatic changes there have been in medical treatment in the last two decades. Some of these are considered price changes; however, they are really quality changes. Health care is a growing component of total national expenditure, so I think we need to pay a lot of attention to the things that we are measuring when we talk about inflation, and the CPI is the wrong measure.

Finally I will advertise something I will discuss tomorrow when we change the subject to international issues. I think central banks, in particular the ECB but I would give the same advice to Japan and the United States, ought to think seriously about focusing on some measure of wholesale rather than consumer prices as the target for economic policy. But part of my motivation in suggesting this is international rather than domestic, so I will save the discussion until a later session.

ALEXANDRE LAMFALUSSY: Concerning the Stability Pact, I would like to mention the following. I have had no part in constructing the Stability Pact, so I have no feelings of paternity in that respect, but between 1993 and 1997 or 1998, the average debt burden in the euro-area countries went up from 57 percent to 70 percent. Now this was a process of a very dangerous speed and size. At the same time, the financing of the deficits, which produced this increase in the debt burden, was relatively easy because contrary to the United States, we have consistently had very high household saving rates. What can you do to stop this process? You have to use a blunt instrument, which is what the Stability Pact is. It does not look particularly intelligent, it is a straightjacket of sorts, but it was the only practical way of stopping a process that was getting out of control.

ROBERT MUNDELL: I think that the Maastricht Treaty and the launching of the ECB were a magnificent success and I think that when you go back to the Delors Report in 1989, it was quite remarkable when that came out, because it was a proposal for a single currency monetary union. It would have been much easier to have an 11 or 15-currency monetary union, but a single currency monetary union was quite a big step, and for a long time I thought that that was too big a step, that European governments would not be willing to accept it [the loss of sovereignty]. But the Delors gamble, and I think it was a big gamble, turned out to be successful and in retrospect, Europe is lucky that it ended up in that direction, rather than with an alternative.

I agree with Alexandre [Lamfalussy], rather than Dick [Cooper], on the issue of the stability pact. I think that there is every reason on the part of European governments to keep on promising more expenditure programs, more social security programs, more spending, increasing the share of government to GDP without being able to finance it. One observed the whole process going on in the 1970s and the 1980s and even starting in the 1960s when the rate of government spending to GDP went up from about 30 percent toward 50 percent and 60 percent. In Sweden, government spending went up as high as 74 percent of GDP, and now they have got it down to perhaps 60 percent. It is a political issue of people wanting more and more programs and it is heading into a budget constraint that is not going to be met because the long-run projected needs, given aging, are going to get worse. If anything, it is not that the Growth and Stability Pact is too strict; it might even be too lax, because it is not just an issue of the debt-to-GDP ratios and the deficits, the unfunded liabilities are also very serious. We have talked about this before at these conferences. There is a growing consensus of opinion that describes a very bleak picture for Europe because of the fact that entitlements and spending commitments are increasing while the opportunities for financing these have gone down, and I support this conclusion.

The euro can do a lot of good things. It is wonderful for Europe, but there are a lot of things it will not do. It is not going to solve the unemployment problem or the growth problem; other policies are needed for that. Today there is a summit meeting in Lisbon, which is taking up these two primary issues – the unemployment problem in Europe and the growth issue in Europe. These issues are becoming recognized, and this is amazing because these reforms are difficult politically, yet are being recognized by left-of-center governments. Consider, for example, pension reforms; people are living until 80 years old or 85 years old and yet in some countries people can retire at the age of 60. It was only a few years ago that a friend of mine told me he is now a retiree, a pensioner, at the age of 55. This type of situation is completely untenable. [Stockholm University economist] Asar Lindbeck, who is a Social Democrat in Sweden and a very fine economist, has argued that the social welfare state is very much overshot, and I think that over the time, these tough decisions are going to have to be made about the level of government spending.

We talk about harmonization – you have to have some degree of harmonization if you're going to have an economic union. First of all, if you harmonize something, you have to harmonize to an efficient system. If one is harmonizing a tax system, one should harmonize to an efficient system of taxes. However, the European Community, as far as I know, has done almost no studies in determining what would be an optimum tax. Additionally, how can you harmonize countries that have such widely different ratios of government spending to GDP:

in Finland or Denmark or Sweden it is 60 percent of GDP, Britain at 40 percent, and Spain at 43 percent. How can you have the same kind of tax system applying to these countries?

Let me make an anecdotal remark. At the royal banquet in Sweden [during the 1999 Nobel Prize ceremony], the king gets to select who his dinner partner is and he selected my wife, Valerie. So protocol requires then that I sit a long way away from the queen, otherwise it would look unfair to the other Nobel Prize winners. So my dinner partner was the Deputy Prime Minister of the Social Democratic government of Sweden, a lady who had had several cabinet posts and was rewarded with the position of Deputy Prime Minister. She wanted to talk about the euro and I said, well what have you got against the euro, why are you so opposed, and she said we are not really against the euro, it is only what we think will come after the euro – once we get involved with this monetary union we are going to have to harmonize tax rates with the other members of the community, and ultimately what that means is that we are going to have to cut down our government spending to the level of the rest of the community. Sweden is at one end of the social pole, and then Britain, maybe Ireland, maybe Spain and Portugal at the other end, all of which have relatively low government spending. Fiscal policy harmonization is an open question; for instance, Britain and Ireland are afraid that they are going to have to raise tax rates, which they would prefer to avoid.

That is the key issue and so what I think the summit meeting is going to come out with is certainly that there has got to be a move in the direction of lower tax rates and deregulation so that you can hire people. No entrepreneur wants to hire people if they cannot fire people. A reduction in the level or the length at least in which unemployment insurance is paid would be an important reform. The big problem in Europe isn't with short-run unemployment. It is the same in Europe as the United States; it's the long-run unemployment that's a problem in Europe. There are countries like Britain with a 4 percent unemployment rate and countries like Spain, which mercifully has come down from 24 percent to 15 percent unemployment. Spain is doing a remarkable recovery, but its unemployment level is still very high compared to other countries in Europe. I think it's quite remarkable that [Prime Minister of Britain] Tony Blair and [former Prime Minister of Italy] Mossiamo Doalema have brought together a plan that involves a lot of these things. Italy has some of the worst problems; they have regulations for everything. Italy has a regulation,

I'm sorry for being personally involved but I have six dogs, and Italy has a regulation saying that you cannot leave your dog alone for more than an hour because someone left a dog alone for 24 hours, it was a terrible thing, and so the government passed this regulation that proposed this kind of law. But if you look through the whole gamut of things in Italy, you'll find there's a regulation for everything and what isn't permitted is forbidden, there's no degree of freedom. There's no kind of monetary system, no macro policy that's going to correct for defects that are the problems of the government's own making.

MAX CORDEN: First of all, I'd like to say the United States has no such regulation concerning dogs as you mentioned, but in the United States of course the dogs would sue the owner. On a serious note, there is a gross economic fallacy prevalent in Europe, which I think everybody around this table has spent time denouncing. The idea is a fixed stock of jobs and that the earlier people retire, the more jobs there are for young people. It sends all the wrong messages. Speaking for myself, who's slightly above the average age of this group, I'm still earning income, I'm not drawing my pension and the reason is that I'm relatively healthier than previous generations. That's why I expect to live longer and that's also why I should be able to work longer. There's no reason why this whole pension problem couldn't be solved by raising the age at which healthy people get their pension. That doesn't stop ill people from getting it earlier. The French government has enforced this ridiculous law. It really shows a complete inadequacy of elementary economics teaching, I suppose, in France and maybe elsewhere as well.

MASSIMILIANO MARZO: I have just a few words to say about fiscal policy. I think the most debated issue here is fiscal policy. I am referring still to the Growth and Stability Pact. This pact says, basically, that fiscal policy, i.e. taxes, should react to the amount of the government debt over the GDP. If a country starts with a debt level that is say 60 percent of GDP and as time goes by the country experiences a shock, which could be a shock to the pension system, what happens? If one does not raise taxes immediately in proportion to the amount of debt that you have to issue in order to pay pensions, then one has erred. Basically, the pact cannot be respected any longer.

My question here is therefore twofold. Given the fact that the European Central Bank and now all the governments [in the EU] have to stick with this rule, this morning Paul Volcker said this works almost as an automatic stabilizer and the question is, how should the European Central Bank set its instruments given the fact that we have this fiscal policy rule? Does this affect the choice of the instrument? Does this affect the choice of the target? Having this rule, does it change dramatically given the volatility of the inflation rate around a given target? These are all questions that should be addressed first of all in theory, as mentioned this morning by Paul Volcker. Since all the previous monetary models evaluate monetary policy rules without taking into account the fact that a government should follow a rule such as the Maastricht policy rule, this is an issue that has to be addressed.

The second question is: what is going to happen if a government fails in this situation? For example, if a particular government like Italy begins to get into real trouble with its pensions, we have a really traumatic situation. What's going to happen if we have a situation where we have to issue a lot of debt and are forced to break portions of the treaty? In an instance like this what will happen to the monetary union? The existing theory is silent on this topic.

Another issue is fiscal federalism. We have a problem in Europe: it's not clear at all if our system of fiscal federalism can support the situation of different countries in different situations with different economic problems. We need a system of fiscal federalism as was stressed several years ago by a number of authors, I recall [UC Berkeley economist] Barry Eichengreen has written a lot on this subject and the Maastricht Treaty does not contemplate this, as far as I know.

MANFRED NEUMANN: I do not understand what you mean when discussing the implications of debt issuance. One does not solve the pension problem by issuing debt. Additionally, your 60 percent problem is no problem because once a country has achieved 60 percent, they can go down to 57 percent and then they will have enough leeway if they experience a shock. I think the debt criterion, once everybody has reached it, would be the best thing.

MASSIMILIANO MARZO: If you have a shock that forces you to issue debt, what's going to happen? That is the question. I take as example the pension situation. You could have a huge increase of European bank interest rates and the burden of interest rates could force you to issue debt.

MANFRED NEUMANN: Mr. Chairman, if I may. The pension problem does not give one the right to issue, for short-run purposes, debt in order to solve some accounting shortcoming. But if one runs into recession, then the commission will decide if a country can do that. One must prove the point.

PAUL FABRA: I am always amazed by the easiness with which free market people like all of us here accept so simply the idea that you have to react to a shock with more deficits. The rules of the game for a central bank or for a government are to exaggerate the trend, for example, to a recession. A government would react in some fashion in order to accelerate the reaction of the people and to get rid of the deficit or the recession and not to counteract.

CHRISTOPHER JOHNSON: I wanted to pick up a few points. First of all, Dick Cooper says that the ECB is not accountable to anybody. It is of course accountable by a treaty to the European Parliament, which has a specialist committee, and is setting up a regular procedure to monitor the actions of the bank. Accountable, of course, means explaining what you've done after you've done it. Nobody pretends that they go and seek instructions from anybody before setting interest rates, but that's not what being accountable means.

Bob Mundell raised the next point I would like to mention concerning tax harmonization. In fact there was a very good proposal made nearly ten years ago by a committee under the Dutch finance minister, Ono Ruding. Ruding put forward a very good blueprint for harmonizing taxes, particularly corporate taxes, in Europe. It fell like a stone to the bottom of the North Sea and was never heard of again. The coming of the euro means that there is once again a case not for harmonizing all taxation, but there is of course a need to harmonize the value-added tax for reasons of the single market and that's being done up to a point without total uniformity; however, there's no need to harmonize income taxes because labor is a relatively immobile [production] factor. The argument really is for harmonizing corporate taxes, because here we see an increasingly chaotic situation in which governments always pretend to foreign investors that their taxes are the lowest in the European Union, while making sure that from the point of view of their own domestic companies, they pay as much tax as possible. The UK government has, to everybody's surprise, come out with proposals that would involve British companies paying several more billion pounds in tax on their foreign operations. So the moral is: if one thinks one can get away with paying a very low amount of tax when one invests in another country, don't worry, the government will come around and claim it through the back door when one has made profits.

At the moment, we have a situation where people are very ill-informed. For example, a lot of people in Britain think that Germany has much higher taxes but they are completely mislead by the top tax rates, which are paid on a very small part of German corporate income. There are so many tax exemptions in Germany that, in fact, German corporations end up paying a much smaller percentage of their total income in tax than do British corporations. So in fact things are not what they seem in the tax jungle. The situation is chaotic; there are far too many double-taxation agreements where governments each try to cream off a bigger share of the profits of their own companies. If we are to have a level playing field, we need a single corporation tax system with similar exemptions for all countries. It doesn't have to be exactly the same rate of tax in each country; that is, in fact, the least important factor determining how much tax companies will have to pay.

I want to pick up Robert Skidelsky's point, because I think it's very important: the question of how much political union is or is not implied by the European monetary union. I'd first like to correct him on one thing that I was always taught in school, which was that the Holy Roman Empire was neither holy, nor Roman, nor an empire. But perhaps we shouldn't push these parallels too far. What I think we want to tell our citizens in Britain is that there is no possibility of a European super state, in other words, a political unit like the United States of America. If we had something called the United States of Europe, it would be a totally different political animal. Each country would still have national independence, but it would agree to pool its sovereignty in certain defined fields of government. We've already done it for trade a long time ago, now we're doing it for money. It may be necessary to have a greater degree of pooling for fiscal policy, but this is currently under debate.

The question here is not do you want to use the monetary union as a kind of lever to create some kind of European political unit, but rather what is the minimum pooling of sovereignty in other areas of economic policy that we may need in order to ensure that this pooling of monetary policy can work effectively. I think here we have two principles: one is that of *subsidiarity*: as much as possible should be done at the lowest possible level of government. We may need broad outlines for fiscal policy, get the policy mix right at the European level, while leaving national governments and even local governments to carry out the details of how they actually raise taxes and how they spend money. This is very much allied to the concept of federalism, which we haven't discussed much, but I think it's a very good concept insofar as it involves decentralization of authority to the lowest possible level – to the states or the cities of the United States, to the national and local governments in Europe. The fact of having a federal structure does not necessarily mean that there is one unitary federal government at the center of it. We can have a very different kind of federal structure in Europe from the one that exists in the United States. We need to bite this bullet, and we should not be shy of the word federalism; if it's properly understood it actually means devolving power to the lowest possible level, which is the kind of approach that will make the European union politically more acceptable to its citizens.

HERBERT GIERSCH: I wanted to come in when Bob Mundell made his fundamental statements about harmonization and the Maastricht criteria. Now, the Maastricht criteria are very good for imposing discipline on national governments, but they also exclude experimentation. One kind of experiment that I have in mind is that we shrink the size of government by first cutting taxes and then using the discipline to explain to the people that we have to reduce expenditure. It seems to me that something like this happened under [President Ronald] Reagan in the United States [1980–88] and I remember that Bob Mundell was in favor of it. I wondered why we have not included it here in his fundamental statement, so I wanted to add a footnote to what he said.

Another point I wanted to make is about harmonization, I wonder whether harmonization is really what we mean. Don't we mean perhaps that there should be differentiation? When Manfred Neumann made his point it was not so much about flexibility, but it was about differentiation of wages according to productivity levels in various parts of the country. If I look at Italy and other countries it's the periphery that has high unemployment as a result of excessive wage equality within the country. This kind of differentiation is really what matters. The larger the size of the country or the larger the size of the union, the greater must be the scope for differentiation, otherwise one gets a distortion in the spatial structure of the economy. The question is therefore how to prevent harmonization in the sense of making things equal, removing differentiation. The idea in Europe seems to be that nation-states are somewhat uniform and that euro-land should be similar to a nation-state. This constitutes the union instead of the diversity that is necessary and has been the great advantage of Europe in comparison to, for example, the United States, where the diversity is in geography and space relative to Europe where it's in cultural diversity.

I wonder therefore whether in thinking about the viability of the market economy we think about competition, that is, competition among enterprises and allowing experiments as a discovery procedure. Should we not have that kind of competition policy also for governments so then governments are encouraged to perform experiments that may improve the situation instead of preventing them by harmonization? For example "small area" experiments, as I have described them with regard to fiscal policy, can pave the way for imitation by others so that others can imitate the success of regional liberalization and deregulation policy. That would mean we have competition among regional units that could serve as a basis for government competition and for making governments more efficient.

RICHARD CLARIDA: I'd like to expand on some points that I believe Richard Cooper discussed earlier. As an economist, not unrepresentative of many in the US, I was ex-ante skeptical of the political viability of EMU, not necessarily the wisdom of it going forward, but whether or not it would be realistic. I give very high marks to the ECB during the first year of its existence. I think that the strategy has been practical, but it's also been the correct strategy, which from my perspective, having studied monetary policy across various countries over the years, I would not anticipate it would need to be modified. In particular, I think the public well understands what the goals of the ECB are in terms of inflation and I think that the members of the ECB have done a fine job in explaining the necessity of looking at a wide variety of indicators to guide policy, given the lags [in the effect of monetary policy changes] that we're all aware of. In particular, I think this applies quite well to the issue over the exchange rate for the euro. Additionally, I think the ECB has done exactly the right thing in explaining to the markets that the goals of policy are aiming at inflation, where the euro and other variables are indicators that need to be looked at, but only within that context. So, from my perspective, things have worked out quite well and the ECB is to be congratulated on a very successful first year.

OTMAR ISSING: After having listened to Richard Clarida, I am tempted just to stop just because this was such a wonderful end of the discussion so far. When he started like that, I was expecting something very unfriendly coming afterward, but fortunately this was the only message; I agree with your conclusion. I think there were so many very interesting contributions, so I hesitate to add that perhaps not all of the problems of the European Monetary Union are solved. I would like to address four issues that were raised.

To begin with, I would like to discuss a technical question: the measurement problem. Due to the measurement bias, we did not publish an inflation range that goes to zero, because to my mind, the danger zone, so to speak, begins early – approaching zero, but nobody knows exactly where. I should add also that this is a new index, which was created at a time when all this discussion about the measurement bias was already underway. It was constructed in a way to deal with many of the inefficiencies that were just discovered at that time. I'm not saying that all the problems are solved, but this index should have a smaller measurement bias than any other. However, further research is needed.

Many speakers addressed the issue of fiscal policy. I think it's very easy to criticize the Growth and Stability Pact from a theoretical point of view. I don't want to defend the Pact as it is, but as a political economist, I think it's better than it looks. It has two major effects on fiscal policy in the monetary union. It should be noted that it [the Growth and Stability Pact] was established at a time when the debt burden had just exploded, and this trend had to be stopped. The question is how do you stop it in a way that is economically sensible and politically feasible? Not to mention the fact that all of the governments had to agree to it. Additionally, it had to be established in a very short period. On a side note, we recently had to write our convergence report on Greece, and if you look to the numbers of Greece, they are extraordinary. There is no country that has come down from double-digit deficits to close to balance in such a short period of time. So in this respect, I think it has worked.

On the other hand I think it was called the *Growth* and Stability Pact for very specific reasons, but I believe that over time if you can reduce the share of government expenditure [in GDP] then it's also a growth pact, but this was perhaps not what the inventors had in mind when they called it the Growth and Stability Pact. This is the working of the pact in the context of stabilization policy, and in this respect, it's too often forgotten that the Pact demands that in the normal period of the [business] cycle, the deficit should be zero or the budget should be in surplus. Everybody is concentrating on the limit of a 3 percent deficit, but the Pact is demanding that a country, in normal times, has a deficit of zero or a budget in surplus. This is what the Pact demands. If a country starts from such a situation and gets into a recession, then it's a long way to go to minus 3 percent in the budget. If it's a very severe recession, then the pact itself has provisory clauses for dealing with that. So saying this Pact neglects the stabilization aspect is just not true.

Thirdly, an issue that was raised previously, the role of the euro as a catalyst for economic policy in general, and the relationship between the monetary union and political union. Prior speakers have mentioned that the main influence of the euro is in financial markets. This catalyst function is now working in a very intelligent way by undermining regulations in many other fields; one sees it in several countries in the monetary union (especially in Germany), for example: mergers and acquisitions, ownership changing from domestic owners to foreign owners, and mergers between different sectors for which different wage agreements are responsible. These developments have strong consequences within the labor market, so reform in the labor market might be enforced via the influence of the restructuring of the financial side of the economy. This, in my opinion, will continue. I think it is, in some respects, just an extension of the global question: who runs the world, capital markets or governments? This is one of the big questions and in this context I think we have also to reconsider what political union means. Consequently, I think organizing our thinking along the lines of the existing nation-states model might be the wrong benchmark when we talk about the political union in the context of monetary union. When we speak of "federal" within the context of political union it means distribution of power to several levels. And the monetary union, I think, creates an arrangement in Europe in which this distribution of power, with checks and balances, might get a new meaning.

The last issue I want to address and this is related to the question of political union, is the role of the central bank. The notion of democratic accountability comes up time and again. The Maastricht

Treaty is the consequence of experience and research. Sovereign nations have entrusted the task of delivering a stable currency to a body that is independent from political influence and not subject to all the temptations connected with elections. I think it was done by politicians who knew about these temptations, and against the background of extremely bad experience. The idea behind this is to have a kind of de-politicized money, because political money is always bad money and, over time, can destroy entire economies. This is the experience. The final accountability of the ECB lies with the European Parliament. In the end, it's the people of Europe, they are the final judges of this arrangement. Our independence certainly relies on the law, you might say on the constitution of the union, but finally I think if the people of Europe don't trust us, if they don't accept our policy, if they think what we are doing is wrong, this arrangement will not survive.

Finally, I hesitate to accept the idea of a form of protection in difficult times for the ECB – protection that is by politics. The experience of the Bundesbank was just the other way around – if there were rough times, the Bundesbank was protected by the consensus of the people. Politicians attempted to take this away. If you read the minutes of the cabinet meetings of 1956 and 1957 when the Bundesbank law was considered, no such independence was discussed; the government wanted it very close and to have a tight grip on it. But the Chancellor lacked the political authority to keep control, because against the background of the experience of Germany with political money, an independent central bank was the only option. It's the people. I think the main challenge for the ECB over time is to get the support of the people in all eleven countries for our policy. This is the final task. Against the background of high unemployment, this is a tremendous task and I think we have to improve our communication to prepare for that day, which I hope is still somewhat out in the future.

RICHARD COOPER: Otmar has touched on the topic I wanted to come back to. Christopher Johnson has said the ECB is accountable. I think it's important in a group like this that we don't have to agree on a report, we don't have to agree on diplomatic language, but we should sharpen distinctions rather than blur them. I used the term "politically accountable." The ECB must report to the European Parliament, one could even say it's report *plus*, because they can be questioned. However, if the parliament doesn't like the answers, it cannot do anything about it and no one else can. This is what I mean by political accountability.

A characteristic of every democracy is that the people who make decisions that affect the lives of millions of others are held politically accountable. In this respect, I think what Otmar said about the Bundesbank is absolutely right; it was created by simple statute. A simple change in the statute could have changed the rules. But the Bundesbank built up credit with the German public, which meant that any Chancellor who attempted to change the statute – weaken it – took his political life into his hands, and that's exactly as it should be.

The same is true in the United States. The Federal Reserve was created by simple statute and the congress and the President together could change it. That fact constrains the behavior of the German central bank and the US central bank. The ECB is not in that situation. It is, if you like, constitutionally protected. I know of only one other country where that is so: Chile. I would make the same complaint about Chile; I think it's a serious problem.

Somebody earlier today alluded to the extreme difficulty of amending the constitution of the European community; so it's not really political accountable. I think this does make a difference. It's similar to deterrence theory in national security; it makes a difference to know that the parliament can change things quite quickly if you get too far out of line with public opinion and it's deeply troubling. It's interesting that the Council of Europe requires democratic accountability for membership, the EU requires democratic accountability for membership, and yet in the Maastricht Treaty, democratic accountability, the standard to which the EU holds new members, is not met.

4. International aspects of the euro

Introduced by

W. Max Corden

MAX CORDEN: We have one hour to talk about the international aspects of the euro. I know I can't really control what anybody does or says, but I thought it would be useful to give a classification so you could at least say what you were talking about, so we have some idea of where your argument fits in.

There are two main issues here: one has to do with enlargement and the other has to do with the euro in the world economy, with particular reference to the dollar–yen–euro exchange rate. Secondly, you could be either talking about explaining some actual events that have taken place, notably the depreciation in the value of the euro, and as well as discuss the future, what you think should take place. It might be useful when you talk to say where your argument fits into this simple taxonomy; it makes it easier for us to follow where things are going.

AXEL LEIJONHUFVUD: My comment is partly prompted by what [Richard] Cooper had to say at the end of the last session, although I may be trampling on your line between the internal and external. What I have to say is the following: when I got into economics in the late 1950s, and for quite sometime thereafter, in macroeconomics one talked about a world that was perceived to consist of a private sector that was unstable and prone to waves of optimism, pessimism and what not. Fortunately in that world, governments were benevolent, competent, and generally wise and they could fix whatever problems the private sector got itself into. Now for the last 20-odd years, the general world that economists have talked about is one in which the private sector will take care of itself and it is the governments that are short-sighted, fiscally irresponsible, time inconsistent and so on. The upshot of this great change in the way the world is perceived has been that macroeconomic policy in the last 20 years has not been about stabilization policy as it was 30 years ago, but rather it has been concerned with, almost exclusively, constraining governments.

It's out of this intellectual background that the problem raised originated; the problem, that is, of creating central banks whose independence is defined in such way that they are not politically accountable. The idea is that they should be independent so that they can constrain the fiscal operations of the government. Now, I think a lot of progress has been made on this business of constraining governments so that we have less to worry about now than we did ten or 20 years ago on that front; however, it seems to me we are back to the old problems. If, for example, and this refers to my comment this morning, one knows that one is in a world where governments respect their intertemporal budget constraints, then one has a good deal of insurance against general consumer price inflation. This will also be a world in which it's possible to inject really large amounts of liquidity in the private sector without causing consumer price inflation but you are apt to fuel asset price inflation. In the worst possible cases, one may create bubbles of the Japanese kind, even if one is watching the inflation rate on the Consumer Price Index [CPI] side.

MARIO BALDASSARRI: I believe that over the last 20 years, European governments made a big push to convince people that they could be better off with less government. Secondly, just because the government is a smaller percentage of the economy does not mean less government in terms of rules and regulations. Governments in Europe didn't do what they should do and try to, in some way, push the central bank not to raise interest rates and not to kill the recovery in Europe. This confusion of responsibility between the central bank on one side, and governments on the other, contributed to the weakness of the euro because the market did not understand economic policy in Europe in terms the of interest rate on one side and fiscal policy and government budgets on the other side. How can we talk seriously about enlargement and about the international role of the euro if we don't know who is responsible for what?

ROBERT MUNDELL: I want to talk about the policy of the central bank from the standpoint of external and internal policy insofar as that can be distinguished. I'm also overlapping a little bit with the domestic program, but there's no alternative to it. There is a general view among the central banks of the world that benign neglect of the exchange rate is optimal. There is no doubt about it; this is a very widespread view. I heard at the Davos meeting, [Guillermo] Ortiz, head of the Bank of Mexico, saying that of all the lessons we have learned from Mexico and all the other [currency] crises, any kind of fixed exchange rate is the worst kind of system. That's the idea, that flexible exchange rates are the only alternative. That's the view that this year a lot of the international monetary authorities are peddling.

Now, what does it mean? What economic theory is involved with benign neglect of the exchange rate? Is there any foundation to it? I see zero foundation to it; zero influences, no treatises written on it, no substantial body of thought has ever examined this question; it's just an issue of dogma. The dogma has come from a view that is often attributed to Milton Friedman, but he doesn't believe it anymore. The view is that clean float of the exchange rate is the best system. [Treasury Secretary 1974–77] William Simon was pushing that view when he was the Secretary of the Treasury – clean floating is better, intervention is bad, and that view carried on. That context might have been correct for the United States at one particular point in time, but a theoretical foundation has never been established for it. I want to challenge that view and I want to challenge, in particular, the view that it is optimal for the European Central Bank to have benign neglect of the euro.

Now think for a minute of not intervening at all in the foreign exchange market; the central bank has to determine the money supply and with that it determines interest rates and a lot of other variables. The monetary authority can change the money supply in either of two ways (leaving aside reserve requirements for the moment): either by buying domestic assets or buying foreign assets. What is there in economic theory that tells us that buying only domestic assets is the correct policy?

There is one case in point where I sympathize with that view, and I think this is the origin of the basic prejudice that current central bankers have. Most of monetary theory is based on the idea of a closed economy. So let's assume there's a single central bank in the world, a world central bank. If we have a world central bank and a world currency, it's obvious that a bonds-only policy is correct, because there's no foreign exchange in the world, one can't buy foreign exchange. But consider a little principality somewhere – it might be Monaco or San Marino, some little place that's got a currency – who would ever say that that little principality should have a separate currency with inflation targeting. I don't think any serious economist would think that. If you have a very small economy in the world, then the small economy would almost certainly fix its currency to a big neighbor or just give up its currency and use another currency. So a very small economy is certainly going to want to be in a foreign assets only policy. A currency board is a foreign assets only policy. Hong Kong has a foreign assets only policy.

What about the European Central Bank? Well the European Central Bank isn't like the world central bank, it's not 100 percent of the world economy; it's about 20 percent of the world economy. Why should you, when you go all the way down from 100 percent to 20 percent, stick with the same policy that would only be appropriate for the world economy? The same is true with the United States, which might be 23 percent or 24 percent of the world economy, or Japan, which might be 15 percent. What I'm really basing the argument on is that the European Central Bank has a set of assets, perhaps half a trillion dollars worth of foreign exchange. What are all those assets doing if they're never going to be used? Why do they need them? Maybe you need them for confidence or something.

What prejudices the view that we should only intervene in the bond market? Why use bonds in open market operations? This is what open market operations are, buying and selling bonds. The standard answer is that changing the price of bonds via the interest rate, changes the relative price of future and present goods, is a very important category of the economy and that provides a justification for using bonds in open market operations. This was despite the fact that at this time, the United States was buying and selling gold at a fixed price, since we were under the gold exchange standard. The same argument can be made for any small country or medium-sized country: The exchange rate has a very big influence in the economy, just as the interest rate has a big impact on spending in the economy. The exchange rate has a big impact on the mix between domestic and foreign goods.

If you think not only about the European Central Bank, but since Otmar suggested that the euro is the successor of the deutsche mark in some sense, look back at the volatility of the deutsche mark and imagine that carrying forward to the volatility of the dollar–euro rate. Let's look at the deutsche mark–dollar rate. In 1975, let's say, the dollar was 3.4 marks; in 1980 it was half that, 1.7 marks; in 1985 it was twice that, 3.4 marks, these are 100 percent changes in this rate; in August, 1992 it was 1.39 marks and now it's two marks. Think of this kind of volatility applied to the dollar–euro rate. Today the rate is, let's say around a dollar. What if it went down to fifty cents? What if it went up to two; either of those alternatives would be terrible for Europe.

I want to make a reference here to someone I admire quite a lot sometimes, John Maynard Keynes. Keynes wrote a very good book called *The Tract on Monetary Reform* [*The Collected Writings of John Maynard Keynes*, vol 4, Cambridge University Press, 1979] in 1923. It made the distinction between internal and external stability. Internal stability meant inflation targeting; the price level was stable. External stability meant the exchange rate was stable, which meant at that time that the gold price was stable (Britain was on a floating rate at that time). He had looked at what had happened to the stability of gold over this period. In 1913 there was a newly created [US] Federal Reserve System. In 1914 the price index, and suppose it started at a level of one hundred; six years later, in 1920, the price index was two hundred. The price level doubled over the avalanche of gold that came in and the Fed monetized it – who knows what they were thinking. In 1921 the price index went from 200 in the United States to 140, a huge deflation in one year. This is all because the dollar price of gold was fixed at $20.67 an ounce. This meant instability in the gold price in terms of other commodities that were equally unstable vis-à-vis the dollar. This is what Keynes was complaining about. Why should we fix our currency to either gold or the dollar when you have this big doubling of the price level in six years, or worse, the deflation of 40 percent or so in one year in 1921? It would be better to stabilize the price level. The important part of his book says internal stability is more important than external stability if there's going to be substantial internal price stability. And then he asks the question, would the US be stable? He thought the Federal Reserve was too immature; there wasn't enough experience in the Fed to have a stable price level. However, he did say that if the Federal Reserve stabilized the price level in the United States, then there would be no need for exchange rate stability. He said we don't know whether the Fed is going to be really stable, they're going to be subject to a lot of political pressure one way or the other, but the best thing for Britain is to concentrate on internal stability; however, as a second priority, we should concern ourselves with external stability, to the extent possible we should manage the price of gold as a secondary objective. I think he was completely correct that benign neglect of the exchange rate, even if the primary object is price stability at home, is the wrong way to go and there is no theoretical justification for this kind of bonds-only policy. Benign neglect of the exchange rate is not a good policy, and if we have anything like the instability of the dollar–euro rate that we had with the dollar–DM rate then it would be disastrous for Europe.

I don't believe the dollar–euro rate is going to be as volatile as the dollar–DM rate. After all, the fluctuations and volatility of the dollar–DM rate were partly caused by the disastrous inflation that United States put the world through in the 1970s when they had three years of two-digit inflation. In 1980 the inflation rate in the United States was 13 percent and then when Reaganomics and Paul Volcker reversed courses and started to stabilize, the dollar soared again. So I don't think we're going to get that, but nevertheless, just looking at the period from the time of the Plaza Accord in 1985 or the Louvre Accord,[2] we've had a lot of instability even in the dollar–DM rate, even though both the United States' economy and the German economy were comparatively stable over that period.

NORBERT WALTER: After those two great statements, mine may be quite minor and Bob did indeed steal my thunder. I suggest that the benign neglect of the European Central Bank will prove to be inappropriate and not helpful and I indeed believe that economists and institutions should consider whether certain market developments are acceptable or not. I just wanted to point to a decision about a year ago by the Hong Kong Monetary Authority that caused the world's economists to blame the Hong Kong Monetary Authority of wasting taxpayers' money when intervening in the stock market. As we all know, after this relatively moderate intervention, the stock market doubled. It's very obvious that the Hong Kong Monetary Authority very wisely put their money where their mouth was and helped not just the stock market but also the international community. I suggest that this is not just a Hong Kong phenomenon; it's a general phenomenon.

Bob just described the wild fluctuations of some exchange rates. Consider a very recent case where BMW pulled its investment out of [British automobile manufacturer] Rover because, among other factors, an exchange rate ranging from 260 to 320 for the pound to deutsche mark makes even the biggest effort of the Birmingham workforce and management not good enough to make this place productive and competitive. So what we caused by these exaggerated developments is

2. The 1987 Louvre Accord was a formal agreement between France, West Germany, Japan, the UK and the US to stabilize the value of the US dollar.

capital obsolescence. We could do better, I guess, and should at least try to do better.

A situation that is characterized by a very weak currency and thus an interest rate that is not as low as it could be may have an undesirable impact on the internal terms of trade. A relatively highly employed international sector might be moving towards over-employment, an exaggeration of its capacity utilization, whereas the fact that interest rates cannot possibly go down implies that the domestic economy is in worse shape. If this is the case for Europe, this of course translates into an even bigger problem for the United States in terms of its current account. The last point that I want to mention, London's praise for a floating currency, may be an interesting invitation to the people in Birmingham to disapprove of the currency union with London.

HERBERT GIERSCH: I'd like to address a slightly different topic, and that is the enlargement process and the role that the euro could play in this respect. I think this is a very important issue for the candidate countries to accession. It's not an easy topic to handle.

The first point I'd like to make is that we should avoid using in this particular discussion the sort of consensus that is taking hold now among a number of economists. They talk about the experiences of the emerging market crises, where one of the conclusions seems to be that most of those countries got themselves into trouble because of the rigidity of the exchange rate arrangements and therefore should opt either for absolutely free floating or for currency board arrangements or anything of that kind. I have doubts about that recipe even for those countries, but I don't want to go into that now, we may talk about it perhaps tomorrow. I have very grave doubts about extending this kind of argument to the accession countries. I think the basic difference here is that they want to join the European Union and with that, sooner or later, the monetary union as well. That is part of the political and the policy objective. I think we should look back and spend a minute or so thinking about the ERM [Exchange Rate Mechanism] experience, which is, in a sense, more instructive from that point of view.

I do remember that when it was decided after the 1992–93 crisis to keep the ERM but enlarge the band of fluctuation to 15 percent; it was almost a joke for many professional economists. In the end, however, it worked remarkably well, and the countries entered the final exchange rate pegging (or fixing) with the central rates. Part of the job was done by the markets themselves, which steered the effective exchange rates in that direction. The reason for that success, of course, was that this was part of a process of building a monetary union and as the political commitment became evident, the downward convergence of inflation rates become more and more valid. The markets saw this before most of the professional economists, i.e. the markets were beginning to see that this would lead to the concentration of the central rates.

Now, I don't want to suggest that for the accession countries the route could be as peaceful and as simple as was the situation inside the European Union. It will be more difficult because they will have quite a bit of trouble in finding exactly at which exchange rate they are likely to be able to join the monetary union; these countries still have a number of problems with the relative price levels inside their own countries: energy prices, public utility prices, and food prices are still undervalued in relation to others. They also have a number of real problems in their economies because their economies "run" at two speeds. These countries, which have received a lot of foreign investment, have industrial productivity that is perfectly at par with the industrial productivity in many countries in European Union. But of course there are large segments of these countries that are not in this situation. So in these cases it is not easy to determine the target exchange rate that they could fix themselves to. It will be a difficult process; but nevertheless, it is something totally different from the situation of those emerging markets that are not planning to join a monetary union. I think one should make a very clear distinction between these two key cases.

CHRISTOPHER JOHNSON: I would just like to remind Herbert [Giersch] that in the first phase of the exchange rate mechanism, between about 1979 and 1985, we had countries like Italy with much higher inflation rates than the average that were devaluing their currencies from time to time in a controlled way, but not accommodating the full extent of their domestic inflation in the exchange rate; they only went about half way. I would submit that phase one of the ERM is quite a good model, perhaps for the ERM II, which will include the Central and Eastern European countries.

HERBERT GIERSCH: Yes, that is happening. The Hungarians have a crawling peg system and the Poles had it, but they want to bend on it. So it is an open question and I think it can be handled. It will be a very difficult case-by-case approach, but certainly very different from whatever situation arises in other emerging market countries.

MANFRED NEUMANN: I would like to come back to the benign neglect issue. The first thing I'd like to say, Bob, is you talked about the swings in the nominal exchange rate, but clearly we should look at the real exchange rate swings and those are smaller than the ones you showed us. That's one thing. The other thing is this: you alluded to the sources of those swings and said: we had this expansionary monetary policy by the United States in the 1970s. Yes, but it was then followed by the expansionary fiscal policies of the United States in the 1980s. I remember very well that the US administration always told the Europeans that the exchange rate was determined in the markets, so why care about it? If you look at the degree of openness in the United States, it is about 9–10 percent; in the euro area is about 14–15 percent, so it's very similar. I think that the strategy of benign neglect is exactly the strategy the ECB should follow, because if you think about it, we have now two big players in the international exchange rate game: the United States and the euro zone. And we do know from history that you don't get a stable exchange rate system if there are two big players or more; you need hegemony. And who has hegemony? I mean, one might say the United States, but this depends on the behavior of the euro zone. It seems to me we could talk about coordination in principle, although I don't propose to do this in practice. After all, it's a euro–dollar exchange rate, so if one central bank decides to do something about this rate, the other central bank or the other country must be of the same opinion, because we cannot have a fight on the exchange rate. If the ECB would signal to the public and the United States that it doesn't take the benign neglect attitude that would bring the ECB into a bad position, because it would permit the United States to run any policies they like and expect that the Europeans will look after the exchange rate. I don't think we want to run into this business.

ROBERT MUNDELL: I just would like to say that in terms of the real/ nominal exchange rates, I think that if you look at the dollar–yen rate over the past five years, the real rate and the nominal rate have displayed about the same amount of fluctuation because inflation has been very low in each case. During the fluctuations in the dollar–deutsche mark [DM] rate in the 1990s, Germany had comparative stability and the United States had comparative stability and yet you do get that shift in the DM–dollar rate from 139 in August, 1992 to 200 today. Now, you propose benign neglect as the best policy. I'd like to ask you a question just to see what model you're working with: Would you have also proposed benign neglect in Austria over the past 15 years before the euro came into being? Would you have also proposed benign neglect to the Dutch over this period? Would you have advocated floating rates for those countries or fixed rates for those countries? Would you advocate that Luxembourg get rid of their monetary union? Under what circumstances do you think that fixed rates would be a good system, or monetary unions would be a good system? If you expounded on this, we'd have a better picture of what your model is.

MANFRED NEUMANN: I would simply say that I wouldn't worry if the United States wanted to peg to the euro.

ROBERT MUNDELL: What would you say about Austria and Holland over the past 15 years?

MANFRED NEUMANN: That was fine from their point of view since they did this because they wanted to have the same rate of inflation on average [as the countries to which their currencies are pegged]; in the long run they wanted to buy credibility. But this is not a problem these days. The ECB doesn't have to buy credibility from the Fed [US Federal Reserve Bank]. On the contrary, if you would look at longer periods, then I expect that the average rate of inflation in the United States will be higher in the future than in the euro area. So I don't see it being rational to peg to the dollar. I can understand that one may talk about smoothing very short run fluctuations in the exchange rate, that is an open question we can discuss, but otherwise, no, a floating rate is better.

ROBERT MUNDELL: What strikes me as surprising in this discussion is that the two economists, who were the pillars of the arguments for floating exchange rates in the twentieth century, [1976 Nobel Laureate and Chicago economist] Milton Friedman and [1977 Nobel Laureate and Cambridge economist] James Meade, completely changed their minds on this. Meade isn't here with us now, but he certainly came to believe in the monetary union in Europe. And Milton Friedman, in a very important article published in 1972 or 1973, argued that the Republic of Yugoslavia should fix their currency to the D-mark because Germany has a better monetary policy than Yugoslavia can or ever would. I've always believed that to a large extent that whenever there's a strong anchor out there, it's always best for a small country to make use of it.

RICHARD COOPER: Bob [Mundell]: What is your view on fixed rates for the United States?

ROBERT MUNDELL: I've never argued that the United States should have a fixed exchange rate. I've never argued that the US should fix to the Mexican peso or fix to the Canadian dollar. The biggest country can't fix the exchange rate. Little countries fix to big, but not the other way around.

RICHARD COOPER: Are we talking about San Marino versus Italy, or are we talking about the US dollar versus the euro?

ROBERT MUNDELL: I'm not arguing that the United States fix the dollar to the euro. I will argue later on that a monetary union between the United States and Europe would be technically feasible, would give both countries a better monetary policy than what they're likely to have with two stable areas that have a greatly volatile exchange rate between them. This way, I'd fully subscribe to Keynes's argument on this point.

OTMAR ISSING: I just want to try to better understand your argument: if you have two big economic areas, for example the United States and the euro area, between which factor mobility is quite limited, with a substantial divergence in the growth rate, with a substantial divergence in the real interest rate, with a substantial divergence in investment opportunities and expectations of opportunities, what is the argument as to why all this should not be reflected in the exchange rate?

ROBERT MUNDELL: Well it's the same argument that if Bavaria has a very rapid growth rate and Berlin has a very low growth rate; that's not an argument for flexible exchange rates. California can go into a big boom and it's going to be handled absolutely optimally within the fixed exchange rate system in the US. People say Ireland should not be part of the European system because it's growing more rapidly than other countries so in Ireland you need to have an interest rate that is twice as high as the interest rate in Frankfurt, or something like that. This is absolutely wrong. Again, think of the monetary area of the United States and the rapid growth rate in California or Florida relative to other rates. The US has the same interest rates all over the place. A California interest rate is the same as in New York and Florida. What this implies is that if the country grows rapidly, more new money is being produced and the other slow-growing regions have a lower demand for money and get less money. Rapidly growing regions have a high demand for money and they get the money that they want. It's the monetary approach to the balance of payments that I thought settled those issues back in the 1960s.

I was in Sweden three times in the past two years, in September 1998 I gave the lectures on the euro and why Sweden should join the euro area. All the economists kept saying 'optimum currency areas'; this was a chant that was going on. I'm surprised that people who refer to my work in 1961 on this seem not to have read it. In the first paragraph it states very clearly that this paper cautions against the usefulness of a system of flexible exchange rates based around national currency areas; it was an argument against flexible exchange rates. Then it posed the following issue: let's suppose that the case for flexible exchange rates, which was classically based on Keynesian money illusions (for example hoodwinking labor unions by devaluing away their real wages in a way that you can't do by lowering their money wages). It is an argument that both monetarists like Milton Friedman and classical economists like Meade believed in. I said, let's suppose that argument is correct, and if it is correct then it can only work if currencies are organized on a regional basis. Then the issue is: what is the region?

The main point of my paper on optimum currency areas was that Sweden should have possibly five different currency areas. Sweden has five distinct regions, Canada has ten, the UK has about four, Spain has about six, and Italy has at least two. If you use that argument in the sense in which it was being presented then within Europe there should be more than one currency among the 11 countries. Every little principality, every little zone, as long as someone doesn't want to move, you have to have a separate currency so that the exchange rate of that country can adjust. The extreme limit of this argument is that every individual has a separate currency so they can devalue it and that is their credit position. Then what do we lose by it? We lose the whole function of money. The basic function of money is its usefulness as a medium of exchange. So this is the thrust of the argument.

MAX CORDEN: Let me just say that if you were able to resurrect John Maynard Keynes and he discussed what he really meant in the *General Theory* [*of Employment, Interest and Money*, Prometheus Books, 1997] and how it would apply now, we'd be fascinated.

5. Lionel Robbins Lecture

Introduced by

Robert A. Mundell and W. Max Corden

Presented by

Lord Robert Skidelsky

ROBERT MUNDELL: It's my great pleasure and honor to introduce this session on the Robbins Lecture. I want to just say a few words about Lord Robbins and then Max will introduce Lord Skidelsky.

[Former London School of Economics economist] Lionel Robbins [1898–1984] was at the first Bologna Center conference and was instrumental in making it a great success. He was the chairman of it for quite some time and ran the meetings in the following manner: he always gave the opening address to sort out the issues that should be discussed, and then afterwards we'd go around the table and discuss the things he said. He came to almost all of the subsequent meetings until the end of his life. Max and I knew Lionel well, I first met him at the London School of Economics [LSE] in 1955, and I think Max had come a year before. I came with regards from Paul Samuelson at MIT and Lionel ushered me into a room for our first meeting and we spent the whole meeting talking about Dostoyevsky's *Idiot* for some strange reason. I hope he wasn't thinking of me. Subsequently I came to admire him very much, and when I came to the Bologna Center in 1959–60 I invited him to these meetings and each year he gave an address. At this time there was a course called European Integration, it was a lecture course that I was chairing, and he attended. Then I saw him again in 1965 when he'd become chairman of the *Financial Times* and invited me to give a set of lectures in London.

His importance in twentieth century economics is quite substantial. Max mentioned his *Essay on the Nature and Significance of Economic Theory* that changed the way in which people thought about economic methodology. Over this period, in the 1930s, 1940s and 1950s, he was the chairman of the LSE economics department and it was during this period that the LSE became a great institution, with people like [LSE economist and 1972 Nobel Laureate] John Hicks and Nicholas Kaldor [1908–86] and Abba Learner [1903–82]. Robbins went on to do many other things in education, business, the ballet and arts with Covent Garden and other things. So it is very important that a few years ago we set up the Robbins Lecture and that's been a tradition of the Bologna–Claremont Conference Center since then. Some of the first lectures were given by [MIT economist and 1987 Nobel Laureate] Bob Solow and [Yale economist and 1981 Nobel Laureate] Jim Tobin [1918–2002]. At the meeting in Mexico, I gave the Robbins lecture.[3] Max Corden is going to introduce our speaker for today, Lord Skidelsky.

MAX CORDEN: It's my duty to introduce Robert Skidelsky. He is professor of political economy at Warwick University. He is a member of the House of Lords, a Life Peer, which is a political appointment. But most important of all, he is the author of a detailed biography of John Maynard Keynes, Volumes I and II that you all have on your shelves [Penguin Books, 1994, 1995, 2002]. Here is the big news: volume III has recently come out. Lord Skidelsky's lecture is on the new financial architecture in historical perspective.

ROBERT SKIDELSKY: Max ended the last session by asking what John Maynard Keynes would have said had he been sitting in that chair. Well, I have to make an apology, I am a very inferior substitute, and also it's sometimes thought that if you're writing about someone you must agree with everything that person says. Well that's not true, I think that Maynard Keynes was one of the greatest geniuses of the twentieth century, but he did not get everything right, and the world has moved on. So what I'm going to say is my own opinion and you must not think in any way it's what John Maynard Keynes would have said had he been alive today.

When I saw Paul Volcker in Princeton two years ago, I had a terrible confession to make to him. I said, "you know I'm really a [an exchange rate] fixer at heart," as if revealing a shameful secret. And he replied,

---

3.   See Zak, Paul J. (ed.) *Currency Crises, Monetary Union, and the Conduct of Monetary Policy: A Debate Among Leading Economists*, Cheltenham, UK and Northampton, MA, USA, Edward Elgar, 1999.

"well that makes two of us in the world." I think there are now many more open fixers and many more closet fixers, people who would be fixers if they thought it was possible. But still, it's a minority.

Most international monetary experts still think that global fixed exchange rates like the gold standard or the Bretton Woods type cannot be made to work because of the inevitable politicization of monetary policy. Any fixed exchange rate system they say would lack credibility. The politicization of monetary policy brought down the gold standard in 1931. This was accommodated in the Bretton Woods system by capital controls. But once capital controls broke down, Bretton Woods, too, was doomed. Since 1973, the rule, or rather the non-rule, has been generalized floating. This is bound to continue, the conventional view runs, because of what [Berkeley economist] Maurice Obstfelt and [Stanford economist] John Taylor have called the "open economy trilemma."

A country cannot simultaneously maintain fixed exchange rates in an open capital market while pursuing a monetary policy oriented towards domestic goals since monetary policy will inevitably remain politicized. And the reimposition of capital controls is impracticable. The major currencies, at least, will continue to float. But here's the paradox: at the same time, it's not doubted that the performance of convertible fixed exchange rate regimes has been superior to that of floating systems, with the Bretton Woods system clocking up the best all-around performance. The years 1950–73 were a golden age of unparalleled prosperity, writes [historian] Angus Madison. Since 1973, the economic growth rate of OECD countries has been half what it was under Bretton Woods during the golden age, and the somewhat better performance of the rest is accounted for almost entirely by the East Asian miracle. Moreover, performance since 1973 has been much more volatile. We've had a "boom in busts." Flexible exchange rates tend to overshoot wildly and generate equally disruptive movements. The East Asian crisis cost the region more than 100 billion US dollars, 10 percent of its GDP, and in political economic terms, as Mervyn King, the deputy governor of the Bank of England said only a few months ago, the sharp reversals of capital flows to emerging markets have caused crises with a frequency and on a scale that threatens support for an open market economy.

Although the academic case for floating [exchange rates] has been severely dented by the post-Bretton Woods experience, attempts to limit exchange rate fluctuations since the 1970s have usually broken down in face of massive capital flows. Mainstream analysis therefore is understandably skeptical about future prospects of any such attempts. Mainstream proposals for reform of the existing financial system tend to concentrate largely on reforming capital markets, making banking systems more transparent and so on, rather than on currency reform. What I want to do in this lecture is to confront the view, represented most notably by [Berkeley economist] Barry Eichengreen that the conditions that made fixed exchange rate systems work in the past have permanently disappeared. I want to argue the exact reverse: that they are reappearing. Of course, no monetary regime is credible forever and any regime may be shocked into collapse. However, as Keynes once said, in the long run we are all dead, and any system that offers better performance than our current non-system for 20 or 30 years is worth serious consideration and some effort to secure.

I'll end with a modest proposal. An important subsidiary aim that I have is to bring together two literatures that are usually separated: the analysis of financial crises and the discussion of monetary reform. My contention is that the missing link in recent theories of financial crises is the nature of the exchange regime itself. But before taking up the main thread, since this is a lecture in the light of historical experience, let me say a few words about the previous fixed exchange rate system.

The two modern examples of working fixed exchange rate systems were, of course, the classic gold standard between roughly 1880 and 1914, though it went on in a way until 1931, and the convertible phase of the Bretton Woods system, which lasted from 1959 to 1971. What made them work and why did they break down? In a way, the classical gold standard is the more interesting case, for my purpose, because it worked without capital controls. It's now generally accepted that it didn't work in the way economists once believed. Specifically there wasn't any automatic adjustment mechanism. Adjustment could be blocked at both ends by the creditor refusing to inflate and by the debtor refusing to deflate. Nevertheless, it worked all the same. Why? Here I follow Eichengreen. His brief answer is because the commitment to currency convertibility was strong, it was not endangered by domestic political pressures and because central bank cooperation supported currencies in crisis. Credibility, though, was less than perfect, especially at the peripheries of the system, particularly in Latin America. Let me touch on all these points.

Undoubtedly, commitment to convertibility was crucially important. To be on the gold standard in the nineteenth century was the mark of a first-class country. To be off it, or to have to suspend convertibility too often, was to be a banana republic. The gold standard was, in [Harvard economist Joseph] Schumpeter's phrase, the ideal to strive for and pray for in and out of season. Countries joined the gold standard to signal their creditworthiness. This was the key to borrowing cheaply and for long periods.

A crucial motive in the spread of the gold standard in the nineteenth century was the emergence of a world capital market. The gold standard was a particularly simple and efficient mechanism for providing information about the creditworthiness of sovereign borrowers. I doubt whether we have improved on it, despite the proliferation of data and credit rating agencies. To stay on gold, a country had to practice monetary discipline, have a balanced budget and be free from the threat of arbitrary regime change. This is precisely the sort of information demanded by investors now. Whereas today, investors must rely on rating agencies and country analysts to provide them with these indicators, gold made them readily available at very low cost.

Secondly, Eichengreen has written about the insulation of monetary policy from political pressure. He attributes this to imperfect understanding of the connection between monetary policy and employment, limited voting, and weak trade unions. This is partly misleading. The gold standard, curiously enough, spread around the world in parallel with the extension of suffrage. In Britain, the Labour Party was its most loyal defender, right up to the moment of its final collapse in 1931.

More important in keeping monetary policy non-political was the relative lack of strain to which the system was subjected. This a more interesting point. It's partly due, I think, to the extent of international price linkages in the late nineteenth century, the high ratio of traded to non-traded goods, the commodity structure of international trade that meant that the wholesale price index was the key index for monetary authorities, and the low share of non-tradable services in domestic GDPs, all of these tended to promote the law of a single price. The price inertia so characteristic of later economies was much less pronounced. As a result, the price levels of trading countries were much less likely to get out of step *ex ante* and require adjustment *ex post*. This is simply another way of saying that countries on the gold standard were less likely to experience asymmetric shocks.

Eichengreen is right to point out that wage flexibility wasn't remarkable under the classical gold standard. But this was offset by a huge safety valve in the form of transcontinental migration. Between 1881 and 1915, 32 million people, or roughly about 15 percent of the population emigrated from Europe; 60 percent went to the United States. Population movements were accompanied by investment flows to develop new lands, the investor and trader following in the footsteps of the colonist. So in all these ways, the classical gold standard up to 1914 was more like an optimal currency area than a collection of national economies. Keynes' quip that the world as a whole has no foreign trade, was never truer than under this system.

Much more can be said about the international political economy context that made the gold standard possible. The main debate has been between those like Eichengreen, who argue that it was a cooperatively managed system, and those who claim that it was a hegemonic system with Britain as the hegemon. Eichengreen is undoubtedly right to say that as far as Europe was concerned, the system rested on central bank cooperation made possible by the relative absence of political conflict. Despite all the tensions, there wasn't a major war in Europe between 1871 and 1914, a period of 43 years. However, Britain was undoubtedly the hegemonic power for the rest of the world, not just because of the extent of the British Empire, but also because of the dominant position of Britain in world trade and the dominant position of London in the international financial system.

To give just one example, Keynes wrote in 1924 that to lend vast sums abroad for long periods without any possibility of legal redress when things go wrong is a crazy construction, especially in return for trifling extra interest. Keynes had Latin America mainly in mind, but for much of the rest of the world it was far from obvious that it was crazy. The United States, one of the largest capital importers, had the rule of law, and elsewhere, imperial organizations safeguarded the investor from exchange risk and guaranteed prompt legal redress [in the event of default]. By 1870, 70 percent of British foreign investment was going to its empire, whose dependent territories were, in effect, on a sterling standard. Even in Latin America, creditors could enforce their will. Something like the international bankruptcy code, now called for by [Columbia University economist] Jeffrey Sachs and others, did exist in the nineteenth century, precisely because so many foreign borrowers were either not sovereigns or if they were sovereigns, they were weak sovereigns. It was thus a combination of economic and political domination that sustained the continuous outflow of foreign capital from the surplus areas of Western Europe to the deficit areas beyond. A system that as Keynes wrote in 1941, transferred the onus of adjustment from the debtor to the creditor, and served at the same time to keep the balance of international payments in equilibrium and to develop resources in undeveloped lands.

Now, I would like to make one a last point about Latin America. It's precisely in Latin America that the limits of informal imperialism became apparent. Political turbulence, populist fiscal policies, unbacked, it should be noted, by any universal regard for democracy, and volatile commodity and food prices made it the most unstable region of the gold standard world. Latin America had frequent defaults, moratoria, capital flights and suspensions of gold convertibility. When the world depression hit the new gold standard of the 1920s, it cracked first in Latin America. It was partly the effect of the Latin American defaults on Britain that brought the gold standard system crashing down in 1931.

In designing the Bretton Woods system [of exchange rates], policymakers were impressed by the virtual disappearance of most of the conditions that had made the gold standard possible before the First World War. With the growth in product and labor monopolies, wages and prices had become rigid. As a result, deflationary shocks produced heavy and persistent unemployment. At the same time democracy increased the demand for social protection, and immigration laws had stopped labor mobility. The ratio of manufactured to commodity trade had gone up and the ratio of traded to non-traded goods had gone down. Private property was under challenge at home and imperialism was disintegrating abroad. The new fiscal and monetary systems associated with Keynes gave the maintenance of domestic full employment priority over the maintenance of fixed exchange rates. So the main purpose of the Bretton Woods agreement of 1944 was to reestablish a global fixed exchange rate system as a precondition for freeing up trade, but one which fitted the new world of political money. The object of an improved system must be to insulate domestic monetary policy not from politics, but from international finance; hence the three Bretton Woods innovations: adjustable exchange rates, capital controls and the IMF [International Monetary Fund].

When the Bretton Woods authors thought about the sources of exchange rate problems against which their system was designed to guard, they thought of four types of problems. First, they had considered domestic shocks. The British emphasized wage inflation with their powerful trade unions very much in mind, while the Americans, with their Latin American experience, concentrated on budget deficits and the monetization of debt. Second were terms of trade shocks. These are particularly important for primary commodity exporting countries. Third, political shocks such as revolutions, socialist experiments, and populist dictatorships, all affect capital flows. Remember that this was done against the background of the Bolshevik Revolution of 1917. And finally, capital flight, which was regarded as a consequence of such shocks and aggravating them, was therefore limited.

Keynes, for example, and this is very indicative of the mindset of people at that time, thought that the position of the wealth-owning classes was likely to be threatened everywhere around the world and that capital flight would be endemic unless steps were taken to prevent it. The remedies proposed by the Bretton Woods agreement were, as I've just said, agreed exchange rate adjustments, control of capital movements, and pooled reserves available through the IMF on certain conditions. But a number of questions arise.

Why did the Bretton Woods architects opt for fixed exchange rates? It was because they were looking backwards. They wanted to avoid the currency wars of the 1930s, and because most economists doubted that floating exchange rates would produce stable equilibria. They thought that devaluation was quite likely to take one further away from equilibrium rather than bring one nearer to it.

Secondly, Keynes succeeded in inserting into the Bretton Woods agreement a clause stating that a country's domestic policies were not a ground for refusing a request to devalue. This was designed to secure sufficient freedom for domestic monetary policy. One consequence, though, was to undermine the credibility of the commitment to a fixed peg. This turned out, for a long time, not to matter. Contrary to Keynes' wishes, the Bretton Woods agreement proposed only minimal conditions on creditors. All that survived of his original plan to force creditor adjustment was the scarce currency clause. This allowed countries to impose an import control against a country whose currency was declared to be scarce; that is, in excess of demand. But that clause never became operative. The reason was that the deflationary dollar gap was eliminated by the American commitment to keep Western Europe and Japan free of communism. This led America to acquiesce in large sterling, franc, and deutsche mark devaluations against the dollar in 1949, and it led to huge outflows of American dollars on government account, later supplemented by large private outflows. These events were reflected in the rundown of the US and the build-up of European and Japanese reserves. The trend in the balance of payments, in turn, enabled exchange rates to be gradually stabilized, and currency convertibility to be reestablished. This, in turn, promoted trade liberalization, which in turn fueled economic growth. So you have this virtuous cycle being established through the voluntary creditor adjustment of the United States, not for Keynesian reasons, but for Cold War reasons.

In 1960, [J.P. Morgan partner] Russell Lefingwell wrote a letter to [reporter] Walt Lipman and I want to quote it because it's interesting now. Lefingwell said the following:

> Wisely we undertook to set the world to rights. We gave money and know-how to our foreign friends. We made fixed foreign investments and we policed the world against the Russians and communist Chinese with foreign bases and foreign-based troops in ships and planes. All this involved spending immense sums of dollars abroad. We and our friends abroad had been so obsessed by the thought of the dollar gap, which until recently, few noticed that the dollar shortage had disappeared and a dollar glut had taken its place. Foreign aid has been successful beyond our dreams. Western Europe and Japan had recovered and were in hot competition with us here and abroad. So our favorable trade balance has dwindled to little or nothing. We are still spending abroad billions more than our income from abroad and the resulting deficit is reflected in our loss of gold and increasing short-term debt abroad. For the first time in more than a quarter of a century, we have been subjected willy-nilly to the discipline of the gold standard.

It had been completely unanticipated that the dollar would be left alone on the gold standard. Interestingly enough, when the Bretton Woods system was set up, people like [US representative to the 1944 Bretton Woods conference] Harry Dexter White and others assumed that the main countries would gradually return to the gold standard, particularly Germany, France, and Britain as they recovered. In France they could certainly have done so in the 1960s, since de Gaulle wanted to. But memories of the old gold standard were too vivid, and the fact that the main gold producers were Russia and South Africa was an insuperable political problem. The result was that the US dollar alone remained convertible into gold; every other currency pegged to the dollar. With sterling rapidly fading out as a reserve and transactions currency, the Bretton Woods world, as Professor Mundell noted in his introduction to this conference, became a vast dollar area.

One thing that America didn't do was to stick to the discipline of the gold standard. Perhaps it couldn't, being incompatible with its political role in the world. Not only was the dollar the world's chief reserve asset, but also the existing arrangements whereby currencies accumulated dollar liabilities, suited the Europeans. The denouement of this might have been postponed had the United States pursued more conservative fiscal and monetary policies in the 1960s. Instead it ignored the 35-dollar gold price constraint and inflated to fund the Vietnam War at the same time as its Great Society [social] programs. The result was inevitable. Once its short-term debt came to exceed its gold reserve, it was forced to suspend convertibility and float the currency. This in turn led to generalized floating in the 1970s.

I want to draw one lesson from this Bretton Woods episode. One's got to remember that the Bretton Woods agreement was a deal between the United States and Britain and no one else counted. The features of the system that strongly differentiated it from the old gold standard were precisely designed to protect a weakened Britain, which felt vulnerable to domestic and external shocks. Today however, when we look at the new architecture, it's not the core countries of the system that need protecting, but the emerging market economies. What globalization has done is to expose the financial inequality of nations. In thinking about a new global financial architecture, therefore, we need to keep in mind the distinction between how the classical gold standard worked at the core of the system and how it worked at its periphery. But I want to take up this point a bit later.

If we look hard enough, we do see the shadowy outlines of a system emerging from the non-system. As someone pointed out this morning, the number of currencies has been shrinking relative to the number of countries, and so you really whittle down the important currencies to three: the dollar, the euro, and more doubtfully, the yen. The peripheral currencies increasingly tend to want to fix to the core currencies both to import credibility and to safeguard trading connections. In other words, the monetary conditions for most of the global economy are close to being set by two or three central banks. With globalization, some of the structural features of the pre-1914 world are reasserting themselves. I think the consensus of economists has been fairly slow to adjust to these developments.

The major agreed-upon intellectual axiom remains that in the presence of capital mobility only fixed exchange rates, as in a monetary union, or freely floating rates are sustainable in the long run. Fixed but adjustable exchange rates like that of Bretton Woods are bound to break down for reasons that Milton Friedman explained in 1953. The advantages of free capital flows are also stressed.

In addition to the usual efficiency arguments, punishment by bond markets is regarded as a much more credible sanction against inflation-prone governments than commitment to an exchange rate target. The great reduction in the world inflation rate since the 1980s is thought to confirm this, though there may be more to this in terms of the classical analysis of financial crises that starts with a structural budget deficit that is monetized and then produces flight from a fixed peg. It underlies the theory of self-fulfilling speculative attacks that was developed to explain the collapse of the ERM [European Exchange Rate Mechanism: a system of exchange rate bands] in 1992, and in their third generation these models can explain the East Asian troubles of the 1990s. The perspective was that it was the fixed exchange rate that severely aggravated the troubles of these countries. The main conclusion drawn from this set of models was not that capital flows should be curtailed, but that currencies should be allowed to float and that banks needed to be more tightly regulated or even foreign owned. Indeed, the attempt to maintain fixed nominal exchange rates in face of capital flight has been widely regarded as an important element that contributed to the East Asian crisis. Following on in this line, there's no shortage of ideas for the prevention and containment of crises in the future.

In his recent lecture, "Reforming the International Financial System: the Middle Way," an echo of Keynes there, Mervyn King, deputy governor of the Bank of England, lists the main ones. On the side of prevention and containment (cum do-it-yourself lender of last resort aimed at providing self-insurance against liquidity crises) either build up large foreign currency reserves on a national or regional basis, or create contingency credit or collateralized loan facilities; manage national balance sheets better; encourage equity rather than debt finance by creating credible legal and institutional infrastructures; design better debt contracts to provide a framework for negotiation between creditors and debtors when facing financial difficulties, and supervise banks better in emerging markets. We've heard them all before. This is the compendium of conventional wisdom: reduction of moral hazard in lending countries to discourage short-term debt flows.

As far as ideas for crisis resolution go, we have an international bankruptcy code; temporary capital controls; greater transparency in public and banking sector accounts, including information about the degree of transparency, which is perhaps a service the IMF could provide. All of these can help both reduce the frequency of crises and their severity. Dr. King rejects two purist solutions: an international lender of last resort and permanent capital controls. The first would create unacceptable problems of moral hazard, as well as being financially and politically infeasible, and the second goes against the grain of promoting market reforms and good governance. All these remedies are perfectly reasonable and are much in the forefront of discussion. I would only make two comments about them.

First, they ignore the possible contribution of the exchange rate regime itself to the financial problems of emerging markets. I use those words advisedly: the exchange rate regime itself, not the exchange rate of the particular countries affected. As two economists, Fred Bergsten [of the Institute for International Economics], and Paul Krugman [of Princeton] have written, it is a debate with a hole in its heart – this whole set of proposals. The dollar rose 80 percent against the yen from early 1995 to mid-1998. As a result, the Asia–dollar pegs led to the substantial overvaluations of the currencies concerned and large trade deficits. This became inconsistent with the scale of borrowing and would have led to investor doubts irrespective of the suitability of the loans being made by the borrowing bank. Most analysts have regarded this as the irrefutable argument for floating, but it might as well be claimed that had the yen–dollar exchange rate not gyrated so heavily, the excesses of the boom and the bust that followed might have been avoided.

My second comment is that all current reform suggestions are rightly targeted on the problem of emerging markets. With the exception of the ERM crisis of 1992, surely an exceptional case connected with the birth pangs of the euro, all the post-Bretton Woods financial crises have been concentrated in Latin American or East Asia. The remedies proposed in current thinking have, except for those pertaining to the reduction of moral hazard among lending banks, been targeted on emerging markets and have little relevance to the core countries of the world economy because they already apply the domestic rules that the international bodies recommend for the rest.

In conclusion, I would like to return to my introductory theme. The current view is that freedom of capital movements goes together with floating and that control of capital movements goes together with fixing. Yet both the efficiency and disciplinary arguments for combining fixing with free capital movements are strong, provided the combination can be made to work. I've given a historical case in which the combination did apparently work. The general case for fixed exchange rates remains as strong as ever. Fixed rates reduce the risks and uncertainties of international transactions and therefore encourage trade expansion and foreign investment. But they've also functioned as a disciplinary device, as a constraint on what Keynes called "the wicked ministers of finance."

The general case for free capital flows is that they increase the supply of investment funds and make their allocation more efficient. However, bond markets also punish wicked finance ministers and reward good ones, thus creating a payoff for good governance, which might otherwise not exist. What I want to argue is that the core countries of the global economy, by which I mean the United States, the European Union and more doubtfully, Japan, are reaching a point when they can contemplate stable exchange rates and free capital flows between themselves with equanimity because their fundamentals are usually sound, their institutions are adequate and they have well-established habits of cooperation. Therefore their pegs will be credible and they will be able to take full advantage of the international division of labor that stable exchange rates and free capital flows bring. Now I agree this is an Olympian perspective that ignores such minor things as bubbles and such that will be problems and they'll occur, but the crucial question that you have to answer is whether they are likely to produce the kind of real effects [on economies] that we saw between 1929 and 1932. On the other hand, turning our gaze away from the core countries, we will find many other countries will be suited to attach themselves to the main monetary centers to get the same benefits. History as well as contemporary practice reveals many kinds of subordinate monetary systems designed to enhance credibility. Currency boards were invented in the British Empire and dollarization is the latest version of that, and of course, there may also be a case for inward capital controls. In short, I reverse the ruling paradigm. Fixed exchange rates and free capital mobility should co-exist – can they be made to?

Let's go back to the gold standard and just reconsider the conditions that made that standard work. Today the conditions are certainly not what they were before the First World War, and I mustn't be misunderstood claiming they are, but neither are they what they were in the fifty years or so after the First World War. We no longer live in the kind of world envisaged by the fathers of the Bretton Woods system – a world whose subconscious influence explains much of the pessimism which still attaches to projects to re-fix exchange rates. Here's a quick checklist. In the gold standard era, labor was domestically immobile but internationally mobile. Today mass transcontinental labor migration has disappeared, but within large areas, such as North America and Europe, cross-border migration is growing and will probably continue to grow.

Second point: in the gold standard era trade unions were weak. Today they are weaker and weakening further. Third point: the structure of the pre-1914 economy made for a large number of direct international price linkages, tending to promote a law of one price [equilibration of purchasing power]. As a result, the price levels of trading countries were less likely to get out of step *ex ante*. This is a point I made earlier in my talk.

Today, are we further away from that kind of world, or nearer to that kind of world than we were in the last thirty or forty years? I would say we're nearer. Consider three factors which surely dominated from the 1920s through to the 1970s in most developed countries: (1) wages were determined by unions, (2) labor markets were heavily regulated, and (3) industry was increasingly concentrated. Economists like [Emeritus Harvard economist John Kenneth] Galbraith drew from all this the conclusion that prices were set by monopolistic bargaining. This situation, which surely captured a moment in history and state of technology, has started to unravel. Changes in the structure of the economy have brought about much more flexible product and labor markets. The most important influences are the huge reductions in transport, communications, and transactions costs, caused by the microelectronic revolution, the rise in self-employment, the growing openness of economies, the rising ratio of traded to non-traded goods, and the growing share of internationally traded services in the trade basket. These developments, which have led to the decline in classic trade unionism, have both cut away at the roots of domestic rigidities and raised the benefits of exchange rate stability. In short, the supply characteristics of modern economies are not exactly the same as they were before 1914, but they are edging back to the greater flexibility of earlier conditions and that puts less pressure on macro policy.

Some of the consequences of these developments can already be seen. For example, under the gold standard governments were indifferent to unemployment. Governments today, or more accurately electorates, are much more tolerant of unemployment than they were. Partly because the long experiment with what I would call "hubristic" Keynesian macroeconomic policy ran into a dead end. Unemployment is no longer associated with the scale and duration of economic downturns like the Great Depression. We are back, that's to say, in a business cycle world, rather than one of permanent demand efficiency.

Under the gold standard, a limited, or more accurately, un-mobilized electorate allowed budgets to be balanced at low levels of public spending and taxation. Today we are, of course, much more democratized than we were under the gold standard. But the demand for social protection has waned, partly because private assets are much more widely distributed. The majority of have-nots in 1914 have shrunk to a minority of the excluded; the change in the vocabulary itself is deeply significant of the change in social conditions. There has been a revival of a belief in limited government. Near-Victorian fiscal rules have been reinstated. The era of rising public spending and large budget deficits seems to have come to an end.

Under the gold standard, monetary policy, insofar as it existed, was discretionary but non-political. It was made by independent central banks. From the 1930s to the 1970s, monetary policy was under the direct control of governments. The result was an almost continual rise in inflation. Today this is no longer the institutional structure. Not only do few monetary authorities now claim the right to choose their own inflation rates, in fact they're all committed to low inflation targets, but belief in low inflation is institutionally reinforced by the return of the apolitical tradition of central banking. Since the mid-1980s the inflation rate has been falling and is now hardly greater than it was under the gold standard. It's not just due to changes in ideas and policy, it's due to changes in the structure of the economy as well, but those changes are, in turn, the conditions for sustaining this kind of policy.

I don't want to be Panglossian about this; one shouldn't be blind to the potential conflict between the growing demand for accountability and the renaissance of the international financial market. For much of the twentieth century international finance was kept under strict national control. Now it's been liberated again. Will there be a similar reaction back to economic nationalism? The answer surely depends on whether international financial markets are seen as benign or malign. In the 1920s they were associated with unacceptable levels of economic volatility. I've suggested that this may have ceased to be a problem in developed countries.

Now, I would like to discuss the last point on the checklist. I suggested that the political economy of the gold standard world supported the maintenance of robust monetary rules. I picked out the dominance of private property, the long period of peace, and imperialism. In 1941, Keynes gave the primary reason for capital flight: uncertainty about the position of wealth-owning classes in the social system of the future. Do we really share that uncertainty today? With the collapse of communism and the end of old-fashioned socialism, the position of wealth-holders in the developed countries of the world has never been more secure. It's more secure now than it was in 1900, because then socialism was a potential; this, however, has subsided.

So what is the new challenge to private enterprise in the developed world? I conjecture that major interstate wars are the primary concern, but much less likely than they were at any time since 1914. In short, the developed world is less prone to major political shocks than at any time this century.

What about imperialism? That's surely gone forever and now we have 190 sovereign states. All of them want to pursue their own policies; if one looks at the world, that may be the formal situation, but it's not the actual situation. Basically, a new western hegemony, or informal imperialism, has emerged, sometimes called the Washington consensus, sometimes called NATO, exercised through fig leaf international institutions like the IMF, the World Trade Organization and so on. Also we're starting to see the reemergence of subordinate monetary systems typical of the gold standard era. This is a source of conflict as well as coordination. I don't know how countries like China or India will fit in, and I don't see Japan looking after East Asia, as is sometimes airily suggested.

Nevertheless, there are these patterns that seem to be emerging. What I'm suggesting is that we are returning to the historic conditions when it will be possible to stabilize the exchange rates of the three main currencies: the dollar, the euro and the yen. Here we have a helpful historical model, the tripartite monetary agreement of 1936, which was triggered by France's decision to devalue the franc. An agreement was signed on 25th September, 1936, in which the United States and Britain accepted a 30 percent devaluation of the franc and the three countries agreed to use their reserves, including gold reserves, to support each other's currencies in the foreign exchange markets within agreed bands. These monetary arrangements spread quite rapidly. They soon embraced the core western democracies. In July 1937, the United States negotiated a series of currency stabilization agreements with Latin American countries. Any such agreement today would have profound implications for the emerging and transitional market economies. The more stable the central rates of the system, the easier it will be for peripheral countries to avoid the mistake of pegging to the wrong currency. However, for such countries there is still likely to be a conflict between fixing and free capital movements, so the best way to make the fix credible is probably through a currency board system, or by adopting the dollar or euro as domestic currencies, and this too echoes pre-1914 arrangements.

I have to confess my sympathies with Professor Mundell's position for a residual link with gold. I would like to see a constitutional role for gold, rather like that of our monarchy, in which the Queen is the ultimate safeguard against madness. I'd like that to happen, but whether it will, I don't know. As a member of the World Gold Council recently quipped, two gold bugs are dying each day and none are being born. Stranger things, however, have happened. I suspect we will have to go through one or two more crashes before we even get as far as 1936, but I feel sure that the route I've sketched is the one to which monetary evolution of the future points. It wouldn't surprise me if euro-land and North America were linked in a monetary union in 50 years' time, except that I wouldn't be around to savor it.

ROBERT MUNDELL: I agree very much with your conclusions but I come to them through a different route. Nevertheless, if we're each going up the mountain who's to say there aren't many different ways to truth. Now a couple comments – these are small or big depending on how you want to look at them.

The basic argument I am making is that the century started off with a highly efficient international monetary system, the international gold standard. That system broke down at World War I, and then it was put back together again in the 1920s in a very bad way that undervalued gold and led to the deflation and depression of the 1930s. Economists then blamed the gold standard for this system and evolved different alternatives to it, particularly the need for national monetary management. Keynes's *General Theory*, which is written for a closed economy, picked up on that and economists became Keynesians. All those textbooks in the 1940s and 1950s are about monetary and fiscal policy from the standpoint of a closed economy. Nevertheless, we went back after 1936 through the tripartite and Bretton Woods arrangements, to an international system. So we had economists pushing closed-economy macroeconomic policies while we had an international monetary system. There was conflict all over the place, and as a result the system broke down.

One could find the way the system broke down in a number of different ways. One is simply that the two principal powers – the United States and Britain – each had automatic sterilization of the external effects of their monetary policy. The system was doomed to self-destruction given this policy. If you have an international system, you have to have international monetary policies; if you have a domestic system, then you're free to do what you want. That is what we did when the system broke down. Basically I think it was a currency area, but there were two views on what the optimum inflation rate should be. It wasn't even so much convertibility in gold because Europeans weren't asking for gold, but rather American monetary policy was too expansionary, too inflationary, and Europe decided to check out of the system and it broke. The Americans then said, after 1971, well at least we got rid of that albatross of gold that has been tying down our monetary policies. The United States then went on a big inflation binge in the 1970s, a big depreciation of the dollar, and then it was during the 1980s that [US President Ronald] Reagan and [Federal Reserve Chairman] Paul Volcker came around and corrected the system and brought back stability.

In the 1990s, we got back to a kind of monetary stability that was very similar to the stability of the first decade of the twentieth century, and with a lot of the same principles: balanced budgets and stable monetary policies. Within Europe, one has a sort of gold standard system in operation, but still there is great instability between the three major [currency] areas.

Where I profoundly agree with you is that we need to make the international monetary system work much closer to the way the euro system works and it could be just as good. We don't have to get hung up on the idea of factor mobility as long as the three areas have a common agreement about what the inflation target and are willing to get together to manage it. Then everything else falls into place. If one does get stability of exchange rates among the three major zones, then international monetary reform becomes simple and straightforward. If one doesn't get this, it won't matter how many conferences people have on reforming the international monetary architecture, they're not going to do any good if you have big swings in exchange rates.

You mentioned the appreciation of the dollar against the yen. For countries that were indebted to the United States in dollars, the real value of their indebtedness rose against the other currencies of the world. I think your lecture on this was wonderful.

ROBERT SKIDELSKY: I just wanted to make one brief comment about approaching the same conclusion by different routes. First of all, being historically minded comes naturally to me. Secondly, I was quite influenced by some of the literature I had been reading on this, and particularly by Barry Eichengreen, who writes more books on this than seems to be possible. Basically he identifies the conditions that made the gold standard work, these were balanced budgets and robust monetary rules; he suggests that these conditions disappeared and that's why we can't go back to a fixed system of exchange rates. I wanted to attack that because it seems to me that the it might do some good by showing the world the main argument for fixing, the model implicit in Barry Eichengreen's account is a fixed price. This is not the model that's most useful to use when thinking about the international system today. I think there are many routes up the mountain, provided we converge in the same place.

ROBERT MUNDELL: I don't want to monopolize this, but let me follow-up. I disagree with a lot of what Barry [Eichengreen] writes. I'm always informed by what he's writing, but I never seem to come out with anything like the same conclusions. I think it's because he's got a faulty idea of the adjustment mechanism. I think he's still in the old mold that a fixed exchange rate system, e.g. the gold standard, bimetallism, whatever kind it is, has to have inflation in the surplus countries and deflation in the deficit countries. In the nineteenth century, one can't find a single example where you get a much higher price level in the UK than in the United States, France or Germany, the major countries on the gold standard. They all had their inflations and there's a business cycle, but prices went up and down at the same rate. There was no way the US price level was going down while the UK was going up. It just never happened.

The other aspect of it that's here is that Charles Reese, former governor of the Bank of France, in the 1920s said that democracy killed the gold standard. Reese was one of the few economists who predicted the depression, and I think what he had in mind by "democracy killed the gold standard" is that you have great demands on [democratic] governments, and then governments are going to want to do things that go against the gold standard. I don't agree that this was the thing that killed the gold standard. It has been said that the greatest fact in modern history was the rise of the United States. This to me is the thing that killed the gold standard – the rise of the United States to superpower status. Already in 1914, the US was three times the size of the British economy and the German economy. In the interwar period the US became much more dominant. I was surprised when I recently re-read Keynes's tract on monetary reform that Keynes has this same basic idea. He said in 1914 that the gold standard wasn't working the way that people thought it was. The stability of gold had become much more a function of the policy of a few central banks. The Bretton Woods arrangements became an asymmetrical system because the United States didn't fix the dollar to whatever gold would be. Gold had become a passenger in the system, a little bit like your Queen is a passenger in the [UK] political system.

6. The future of the EMU, the euro, and international finance

Introduced by

Richard Cooper

RICHARD COOPER: First, is it the aim of Europe that the membership of the EU [European Union] and the membership of the EMU [European Monetary Union] should be identical? Is that an objective or not? If so, what are the principles that will govern the choice of an exchange rate for a new entrant? It seems to me that this is a very important point that we have not touched yet on.

The second issue has to do with the role of the euro beyond Europe, beyond the EMU. There are aspirations within Europe of an international role for the euro. The first question is why are there such aspirations? What steps need to be pursued in order to achieve that aspiration? What are some of the consequences of success in attaining a worldwide role, that is to say a role outside of Europe for the euro? The questions lead us into the topics this morning: the general role of international reserves, diversification of portfolios to different international reserves, and so forth. So I invite a conversation to begin on those topics.

Before I finish though, I want to say I was on the list as somebody who wanted to speak when we ran out of time yesterday. At your places, I've circulated a paper that I did for a conference sponsored by the Federal Reserve Bank of Boston, and it came out a few weeks ago in a book called, *Rethinking the International Monetary System* [Jane Sneddin Little and Giovanni P. Olivei (eds) (2001), University of the Pacific Press]. That paper has the usual fluff that we academics put in our papers, background and all of that. There are two thoughts in the paper, one that reverts to the trilemma that Robert Skidelsky talked about in his Robbins Lecture last night as it applies to developing countries. The trilemma as he has described it, and Bob corrected him, but not completely appropriately in my view, is that a country cannot pursue monetary policy, fixed exchange rates, and full currency convertibility at the same time. That's the incompatible triangle. The observation in this paper is that a country cannot pursue independent monetary policy, full current account convertibility, and floating exchange rates. I'm not talking now about all countries, but countries with poorly developed capital markets. That's not on our agenda today, but I thought I'd mention it.

What is on our agenda was the question raised by Otmar Issing: What is the case for fixing exchange rates? He expressed genuine puzzlement that there was so much enthusiasm by some of our speakers for fixed exchange rates. This paper makes a conjecture that tries to answer that question. The observation is that flexible exchange rates are indeed a shock absorber for dealing with what we now call asymmetric shocks among countries. They are also a vehicle for transmitting disturbances from one economy to another, and in particular, disturbances that arise in capital markets, mediating through exchange rates that are not tacked down. The conjecture in the paper is that as we move forward in the next two decades, the ratio of disturbance transmission to the shock absorbing character of flexible exchange rates will rise and at some point will cross a level that's unacceptable. So people like Paul Volcker, Robert Skidelsky and Robert Mundell are ahead of their time, but their time will come.

ALEXANDRE LAMFALUSSY: I will address both questions, and then I'll keep quiet.

The first concerns the accession countries. The answers to your specific questions are relatively simple. Yes, once you are a member of the EU, you have an obligation to try to join the EMU. There is only the UK, which had an opting out clause, and Denmark, which had an opting in clause; all the others have an obligation to try, and once they comply with the criteria, they must join. That is quite clear. What is also clear is that once you are a member of the EU, and you are in the queue for joining the EMU, you are supposed to be part of ERM [exchange rate mechanism] too. The arrangement still applies; it applies to Greece at present. This is the legal or constitutional aspect.

The real problem, as far as I can see, for these countries is not so much what they are going to do once they are in the union, but what they are going to do between now and joining the union. This is not yet settled. They are already taking the euro as an anchor currency, but what does that actually mean? You have a narrow band, a wide band, you have a crawling peg, or no crawling peg, and this choice is left open for debate.

I now turn to the second question concerning the international role of the euro. There's no one here from the European Central Bank [ECB], but Otmar Issing would have told you that the position of the ECB is a neutral one. They have no ambition for the euro to become an international currency; no central banker in his right mind definitely wants to have his currency used internationally, because it has some advantages, but also quite a few drawbacks. So there's no official desire or commitment, but they are not against it either.

Having said that, what are the basic preconditions for the euro to assume an international role? Clearly, the appropriate policy of the ECB is [price] stability. The more important condition, which is a very practical one, is the development of a euro-denominated public debt market that is liquid, deep, and allows the holders of euro-denominated assets not only to get in, but also to get out. This is the point that was made by Giorgio Basevi. The fluidity of entry and exit into trading markets has been advancing very quickly. Progress on the side of the issuers of government debt can still be improved. For example, how to harmonize the nuts and bolts of issuing techniques, whether you pay your interest on a quarterly or half-yearly basis, and how you actually calculate the yields must be worked out. It's very important so that in the end, once we have a market, the only yield differences that appear between say, Italian debt or Belgian debt or German debt, are credit risks.

RICHARD COOPER: Taxation?

ALEXANDRE LAMFALUSSY: Taxation can also be included in these reforms; all that has to be done. How fast will these happen? On the side of the issuers, I don't know, but they are very much aware of it. There is pressure, a sort of competition to issue one's own debt. Governments are really forced to cooperate in this field, but it is a very slow and difficult process.

NIELS THYGESEN: Let me add a few words about both topics, first on the enlargement of the EU. It might be interesting to reflect on a scenario for enlargement. We should keep in mind that the applicant countries seem on the whole to be highly interested in joining the EMU at the earliest possible stage, even to the point where some recent papers by the European Commission have seen it necessary to warn them against haste in this matter and stressing that they should complete their adaptations to the internal market as a first priority. The political wish is there, and given the structure of the commitment, no one would deny a country that really wished to go for EMU. If we look at the data and the schedule for enlargement negotiations, it seems that the earliest time one could conclude these negotiations for membership into the EU is the beginning of 2004. If we then apply the two-year rule that Alexandre Lamfalussy referred to, 2006 might be the first time for entry of a new country; some of them will, no doubt, be ready at that time. We have two countries among the applicants that already have currency boards, pegs to the deutsche mark, and a number of others that are quite advanced at stabilizing their currencies against the euro.

If we look also as an illustration at how far some of the present members of the EMU were from having met the Maastricht convergence criteria about six years before they joined, you will conclude that in a number of respects, the new applicant countries are better qualified according to the Maastricht criteria than were the so-called "club med" countries. Their government deficits, in particular, are much lower. Their inflation rates are still somewhat high, but not much different from what they were in the "club med" countries. Public debt ratios are much lower, on the average about 30 percent of GDP. The crucial issue is whether one can reconcile the inflation criteria, of having an inflation rate that is no more than 1.5 percent worse than the best three performers in Union, with the requirement of having a stable exchange rate. That hinges very much on whether you believe in the kind of Samuelson effect that would affect their inflation rate as measured by consumer prices in this catching up phase. These countries clearly face a trade-off.

I believe that it is time to think very seriously about a substantial expansion of the euro area in terms of membership, not in terms of the size of the economy, but certainly in terms of the numbers. This will pose problems for the functioning of the European Central Bank, given the kind of voting procedures that are presently in place. In a way it would have been logical for the intergovernmental conference this year to already start looking at the adaptation of the ECB to this new membership structure.

VÁCLAV KLAUS: First, my point is that the entry, or the enlargement, is and will be a political decision. It will not be decided in conferences like this one. It will be decided at the moment when the political bosses of Europe will decide that it's necessary to accept new members and especially when it is *possible* to accept new members. It is quite clear that when we talk about sequencing, there must first be EU institutional restructuring. Only after that can there be enlargement of the EU. I don't know when that will be done; it will probably not be tomorrow. We are economists, some of us econometricians, so we study time series. But, making forecasts based on past experience shows us that there is a very interesting empirical rule. The moment of entry is the day you discuss it, which means (today), 25th March, plus seven years. That's the empirical rule. For me to discuss the exchange rate arrangements after entry is a theoretical question, which is not that interesting for a politician of the country involved. That's my first comment; it will be a strictly political decision.

My second point is that I don't think it is a free decision as to what kind of exchange rate regime to accept. The question is different; it is something like what we would call the natural rate of inflation in a transition country compared to the natural rate of inflation in a standard European country; I think these two values are different. The natural rate of inflation in a transition country is visibly higher, and an attempt to suppress inflation below the natural rate is very dangerous as it happened in my country in the last two years. We had zero inflation or maybe disinflation for some time, and as we all know, the costs of disinflation, of rapid unnecessary disinflation, may be very high and it was very high in my country. We have the European inflation now, but at an enormous price in terms of lost output and income. The question is what's the correct sequencing? Will participation in the EMU speed up the processes of transition, or will it block it? That's the economic issue, but again as I say, the enlargement will not be done tomorrow, so we can very easily postpone discussing those things until our next conference. It doesn't mean that there is any alternative for our membership in the EU, no there is no alternative, but I don't think it's a forthcoming issue. On the other hand, when professor Lamfalussy mentioned the ERM II, I can very easily imagine that we [the Czech Republic] will not have any bigger problem to join such a regime than Greece, for example. Greek inflation is probably higher than our own, and the fluctuations of the exchange rates are smaller in our country. So I can very easily imagine phasing out big problems to enter such an arrangement quite easily.

RICHARD COOPER: Can I ask a technical question about ERM II? In ERM I, up until 1987, there were, in fact, exchange rate changes roughly once per year for the first eight years of the European monetary system. Is it envisaged that in ERM II there may be exchange rate changes?

PAUL FABRA: Yes.

RICHARD COOPER: And there is a provision for that?

OTHERS: Yes.

VÁCLAV KLAUS: If I may add a point on the bands in that arrangement. Consider my country and the devaluation done on 29th December 1990, two days before D-day [price liberalization, and foreign trade liberalization]. We theoretically could have had complaints [from EMU members]. But since that time our exchange rate vis-à-vis the German mark is unchanged. So we can very easily participate [in the ERM II].

RICHARD COOPER: Yes, but the Czech Republic may not be entirely typical in that respect.

ROBERT BARTLEY: I just wanted to make a brief point on the question of exchange rates in transition economies. Looking at our housing allowances in Hong Kong, I once asked John Greenwood to write an article explaining to me how, when the Hong Kong dollar was linked through a currency board to the United States they could have more rapid inflation than we did, very noticeably more rapid inflation. The answer was basically that with limitations on immigration, the increase in the Hong Kong cost of living represented people getting rich.

RICHARD COOPER: It is noteworthy that the Japanese yen was tied to the US dollar for twenty-two years at a constant exchange rate, and throughout that period Japan had a higher rate of inflation than the United States as measured by Consumer Price Index, and when the exchange rate changes finally came, the Japanese yen appreciated, not depreciated.

ROBERT MUNDELL: I think that the Hong Kong explanation and also the Japanese explanation, particularly the Japanese appreciation in the 1980s and 1990s, is due to very rapid growth in productivity in the international or traded goods sectors. That means that the real exchange rate has to increase in those cases. If you look at the Hong Kong experience, with a fix to the dollar at 7.8 Hong Kong dollars since 1983, the real exchange rate soared in Hong Kong over that period because the domestic price level rose more rapidly than in the United States. In Japan, you had a similar phenomenon and a similar cause, very rapid growth in the international goods industries, and appreciation of the yen.

ALEXANDRE LAMFALUSSY: The practical problem for the transition countries is that there is likely to be a real appreciation of their currencies in terms of consumer prices. There is no doubt about that, and it is bearable as long as there is no real appreciation in terms of labor costs. Therefore it all hinges on the rate at which productivity increases in relation to labor cost increases. This is important because if they do not have a real appreciation in terms of consumer prices, they will never catch up in any sense in terms of real income.

ROBERT BARTELY: In the case we just talked about here, as long as the exchange rate is stable, why should we care about inflation rates?

ANDRÉ SZÁSZ: I think you rightly pointed out a while ago that the Czech Republic and similar countries are not the main problems in the case of widening [increasing the number of countries in euro-land]. The problem is that it is unclear at the moment how far widening is going to go; nobody has a concept there. The only thing that we know at the moment is that there is a tendency, on the one hand, to be quite strict on the convergence criteria on paper, but to politicize them if there is political reason to do so, and there usually is. The question then becomes, how heterogeneous can a territory with a single currency become without having repercussions on how it functions?

If I look at the present EU, I can only remind you that we started out, not only with wide divergence economically, but also with divergent traditions and policy views. It took some thirty years of informal, but increasingly close cooperation to make those views converge. Even so, personally I'm quite convinced that the treaty, as it is, would be quite different if it wouldn't have been for the dominant position of Germany who forced the other countries' hands. Neither the quantified budget criteria, nor the independent central bank would be in the treaty in this form. It took 30 years, more or less, to accomplish this, yet the underlying views are still way off from what we agreed to on paper. If I look at widening, and again I repeat it's not the Czech Republic, it's the further widening where we don't know where it stops, but rather we lack thirty years of informal cooperation enabling us to converge in the ideas. I'm not arguing that there is an alternative here; I only say that we shouldn't assume too easily that there would not be problems in the future. In fact, I think there will be.

NORBERT WALTER: First, I'd like to stress that the Maastricht Treaty [the specifying process for entrance in the monetary union] probably has misled us to focus too much on macroeconomic convergence. We have probably underestimated the problems that are a result of the microeconomic setting in many of these countries. In particular, the financial sector is anything but developed in quite a few of them. I do not know what this implies for the euro-land if we enlarge, and we should look into that with much more detail. That's one element.

The second element is that I believe that Václav Klaus is correct, that [EU enlargement] is a political process, and that political process is very asymmetric. Whereas Western European countries obviously show a lot of hesitation to admit new members, it is obvious that many countries that are trying to join are progressing and have advanced towards entering euro-land. We see the currency board development on the one hand and we see policy convergence in many other cases. Even if Western Europe is unwilling to address the issue, I think we will be confronted with the use of the euro in much of Europe quite soon. We should consider economic policy, and the political implications of exactly that.

So to address the issue that Václav Klaus mentioned, understanding the institutional arrangements needed to fit a Europe of 25 or 28 [countries] is very important. I have yet to hear, for example, how we deal with 28 central bank governors being members of the council of the ECB – we have not addressed the issue of whether the number [of countries in the ECB] should stay as it is today. What would this imply, if there were no changes, and what are probable solutions for a council that remains workable? I would like to address this issue and have open and frank discussions about it so that politicians have some ideas of how to go about it.

RICHARD COOPER: Let me tell a story. We have a constant stream of senior European officials coming through Cambridge, Massachusetts, and one of them, from a small member of the EU that shall remain unnamed, simply asserted that his country, and he thought he spoke for several other small countries, would never, never, never give up seats as governors [of the ECB]. If this is deemed to be an important issue for small countries, I think Václav Klaus' rule of today plus seven years can persist indefinitely into the future. Then Norbert Walter's speculation that Europe will become "euroized" *de facto*, long before it becomes "euroized" institutionally becomes a live issue and one has to think about the implications.

VÁCLAV KLAUS: If I may make a very small point: the same is true for the new member countries. The idea that there are too many governors and that a country after 50 years of communism would give up its sovereignty and enter the EU and then they will decide, for example, that there will be one commissioner for the Czech Republic and Hungary. It is absolutely impossible to accept anything like that.

RICHARD BLACKHURST: The WTO represents the logical extension of this, to the point where you now have 136 members, on the way to about 165. And every council in the WTO is open to all the members. There is nothing like the executive board in the [World] Bank or the IMF. The idea that there would be a board with, say, the big three having their own seats and the remaining 160 or so countries sharing the seats, just gets blocked. It is actually the most serious internal problem facing the WTO at this point.

GIORGIO BASEVI: I think that focusing on the implication of widening the euro-area may be misleading. Again, I think the de facto situations will really matter more than the actual institutional widening. There was an interesting speech given recently by [European Central Bank Vice-President] Christian Noyer of the executive committee of the ECB that puts forth the idea of time zone currencies. I think this is suggestive of what will happen. It's not just the widening of the EU, but it's really the time zone that is more or less around the Central

European meridian that matters. Why does it matter? It matters for the reasons I put forth yesterday. That is, in the end, markets do not work 24 hours a day, because you need surveillance, you need regulation, you need settlement arrangements, you need control, you need a lender of last resort and this, in the end, acts on the basis of a certain time in the day. So, there are markets that geographically orient to the domain of a currency. This fits in a way with the idea of the three main currencies – the euro, the yen and the dollar, except it's not that clear that the yen will capture the large time zone that goes from Sydney to Singapore. For the euro it's much easier. Then the critical question is: Where will Russia go? This links with the price of oil, and forces us to consider, in which terms will oil be denominated in the future? Still in dollars, or perhaps in euros? Where will the Arab countries, the oil producers of the Gulf, go? This is more important in my view than the institutional enlargement of the EU. In other words, how will the time zones starting from Moscow and ending in Lisbon affect the use of currencies? This goes down to South Africa, by the way.

EMIL CLAASSEN: I would like to consider a few points discussed by Giorgio Basevi. Singapore has a currency board, but with a floating exchange rate. This is probably the best example of what we have in our list, not so much Hong Kong. A full currency board implies that M3 [cash, current account deposits in banks or savings institutions, savings, and time restricted deposits] is nearly covered by international reserves. This is not comparable to the transition countries because there is no labor migration into Hong Kong and into Singapore. A very important point is labor migration that turns up in the East European context. The question of how to settle that down is important and so I suggest a gradual, monetary integration into the euro area. Then we have the second step, the Maastricht Treaty, in one interpretation or another. And then if everything goes okay, you can replace your local currency by the euro. This is the conventional wisdom.

Another fundamental issue is migration as it was with the monetary unification in Germany. That migration can only be solved indirectly by having capital inflows. Capital goes in and then the marginal product of labor goes up to generate equalization between the wages in Western and Eastern Europe. I think capital flows more easily if the country is highly macro-economically disciplined. Why shouldn't one shorten this process? The transition to a currency board, and then to a full "euroization" is at least one other scheme.

MARIO BALDASSARRI: I cannot give an answer to the enlargement question if we cannot give an answer to these three questions, which are: how far east, how far south, and how fast? The first question is not concerned with price and financial stability, but rather with growth, full employment and welfare. If we put together these three questions, I do believe that enlargement depends upon [capital] deepening. As far as the euro-eleven countries, they have to show that the euro is the base for growth and full employment. To be able to put the euro in an international context and in an international role, a currency must be able to provide stability and growth. In this case, I do not believe that deepening inside the euro-11 or the [EU] 15 in some way should go together with enlarging, because enlarging is the aim to reach the results that the first group of 11 can reach by deepening.

MANFRED NEUMANN: I think there is a deep political problem with enlargement and I am even more pessimistic than Václav Klaus, because the size problem is very important. The question is whether the voting should also depend on relative population size. This, of course, will give Germany a larger share, and that is a problem for countries like France. On the other hand, a country like France realizes that if you continue the way we have written the rules so far, then the large countries might be dominated by a coalition of small countries, although it is more difficult to get a coalition of many participants. This is a threat to the Franco-German leadership in the EU. So one has to think about how one can continue this way in a larger European Union. This is a difficult problem, and no one has really come to grips with how to do this.

It is easier for the ECB than it is for the Commission. For the ECB we can at least in principle discuss districting. We can look to the United States and in principle we can have two types of solutions in this respect. First, we could try to unite some central banks to work together with the smaller countries, for example, the Dutch and the Belgians. Then we could say they have a joint seat, and they might decide among themselves who takes the seat every five or eight years. On the other hand, we could keep all national central banks and say, well your country via your governor can vote every 20 years. This is why the large countries, of course, claim that their governor has to have a seat at all times. This really is a problem.

With respect to the executive board of the ECB, it is clear that we have to move in the direction of de-nationalization. It should not be important from which country somebody comes who sits on the executive board. The president, of course, realizes the political issue, but we first have to start with the other positions on that board. If we realize that equality is important, then this might help in general. With respect to the EU Commission, let me make the strong statement that I made already at the time when we had twelve members: it was too large. If you look at the business distribution among the commissioners, it was hilarious, because there were at least three commissioners who dealt with foreign policy issues, for example. There was no clear principle; everybody wanted to have a share of the power. So what is the solution? I do not think that we can move forward in this way. On the contrary, we have to shrink. I could imagine a Commission of ten people with clear mandates as to who attends to which type of policy, but I do not know how to select them, of course.

MATE BABIC: Let me go back a little bit to the problem of the admission of transition countries to the EU. There are several facts that can explain why this process is very slow and I think it will be slow, so I agree completely with Mr. Klaus. Some of the candidate countries have complied completely with the Maastricht criteria. Croatia for example has fulfilled all of them since October 1993 with a rate of inflation averaged around 3 percent; their budget deficit was lower than 3 percent every year, and government debt is lower than 60 percent of GDP. So it doesn't matter whether you fulfill the criteria or not, the most important issue is a political one.

The fact is that most of the currencies of these countries have already been pegged indirectly through the deutsche mark to the euro. In that respect, there would not be much change. In some of the countries, particularly in my country, since the early 1960s when the first wave of *gastarbeitern* [guest workers] went from Croatia to Germany and they started to send remittances in deutsche marks, there has been a parallel currency in Croatia. Additionally, 90 percent of the savings in Croatia are denominated in deutsche marks, so the facts, I think, speak for themselves.

There are some other problems that may make the problem of admission more difficult for these countries. First, almost all of them, except maybe Poland, are small countries. Their interest to join the EU is much greater than the interest of the EU to accept them. Second, the transition countries are relatively undeveloped and the EU is the rich countries' club. I'm not quite sure that they would be willing to accept countries with US$5000 per capita income because that could put pressure on the funds of the EU for faster development of the relatively undeveloped countries. There are economic reasons for the political solution of these problems. We cannot expect that the admission of the new countries, especially the former socialist countries from Central and Eastern Europe, to the EU will be very fast. They have to try to fulfill the Maastricht criteria and to try to speed up their own growth as much as possible in order to fill the gap in a reasonable time. The question is whether they can do this. They lack the capital. They have relatively undeveloped financial markets, they need quite a lot of help, not only advice, but real help in order to speed up their process of development to qualify for admission.

ENZO GRILLI: I would like to mention one observation on the reform process of the EU commission. Let's not forget that the driving force of the institutional changes is not the enlargement of the EU, but it is the deepening of the EU; these considerations drive the process. I'm not saying that the two processes are irreconcilable, but emphasize that it is the necessity of making the EU, the euro, and in particular, the monetary union, workable. This constitutes the biggest push towards institutional reform.

The second point is that for the economies of the countries of Central and Eastern Europe, the choices vis-à-vis the EU are already made. These are small economies with a fairly large share of trade with the EU. They face shocks that are of the same nature as those that the EU faces, at least externally. For them, credibility is important, and inherited inflation is a problem. They do not really have any other possibility given the existence of a large monetary area, but to join in *de facto* and actually peg to the area.

MARIO BALDASSARRI: Just to clear a point raised by both Mate [Babic] and Enzo [Grilli], is it better for these countries – small, open economies – to fulfill the Maastricht criteria and maximize growth to catch up faster? My question to you is, is it better to have ten years of ERM and then enter the EMU as we did during the 1980s, or is it better to enter the euro immediately?

MATE BABIC: I think it would be in our interest to enter the euro as soon as possible, but I do not see any chance for the next seven years, or even more.

VÁCLAV KLAUS: May I make one comment. I don't think that the participants here know the substance of our association agreements with the EU. For example, take my country [the Czech Republic], trade relations will be settled finally as if being in the EU as full members in the year 2002. This occurs because of the association treaty, regardless of entering the EU. This is something that is probably not known.

RICHARD COOPER: Is this including or excluding agriculture?

VÁCLAV KLAUS: Excluding agriculture, this is not a problem for my country.

RICHARD COOPER: That's not important for your country, but it is very important for some of the other applicants.

PAUL FABRA: A short remark about what Mr. Grilli said. I want to also insist on the confidence we should display vis-à-vis the pragmatic aspects of the institutions, and evolutionary aspects of the common market in the EU. It has always been a pragmatic evolution, a Darwinian evolution, and I think that's what we should encourage. However, what we should discourage very strongly is to have these ideas, which are developing nowadays in the academic and the political establishments, put in stone. There is nothing more dangerous in a nascent confederation than to put institutional and other arrangements in stone and then not to be able to adjust them to the circumstances 20 years later.

HERBERT GIERSCH: Let me draw your attention to a point that has been mentioned several times. This is the question of factor mobility between the old Europe and the enlarged Europe. There's not only work to be done within the countries that want to join, but also work to be done in terms of the countries that form the EU so far, particularly at the frontiers. We have wondered why joining East Germany and West Germany created such high unemployment problems, because monetary unification was considered to be a way to equalization, particularly of wages. I have asked Václav Klaus how he, in the early days, managed to keep the wage level so low in the Czech lands as compared to the neighboring countries such as Germany, and other high wage regions. This means that there are several problems to be solved in these markets.

To begin with, we must consider the enlarged flow of capital from the western and central regions to the newly joining countries. This requires something to think about – property rights and the rules against the acquisition of land by Germans, for example, in Poland. I don't know how it is in the Czech lands. On the other hand, it requires the western parts of the euro zone to be enlarged, that there is more differentiation, particularly with regard to wages. Consider the danger of excessive factor mobility and factor movements from the periphery to the center of the European system. This fear needs to be reduced, but it requires that the EU, in preparation for the enlargement, adopts the kind of differentiation with regard to wages and perhaps also other variables that are necessary for making the enlargement work. This means institutional reforms. Here I want to stress institutional reforms with regard to the foreign direct investment in the capital markets of the newly joining countries, and also with regard to adjusting the labor market conditions so that there is a smooth integration with [wage] differentiation, rather than integration without differentiation, which created the huge transfer problem for Germany when East Germany joined West Germany.

CHRISTOPHER JOHNSON: We shouldn't forget that the original impetus behind enlargement was a geopolitical one. When the Soviet Union moved out of Central and Eastern Europe, there was a vacuum that western leaders felt had to be filled. Joining NATO has been part of the solution for the countries furthest away from Russia. Clearly it is not going to be the solution, for example, for the Baltic republics and the territories further east. For them, the way of integrating into the western family has been enlargement. Since Russia became a much weaker country, I think that political impetus to go ahead as quickly as possible with enlargement, for example, as quickly as the unification of Germany, has been lost. Watch Mr. Putin, he has a rather different view of the importance of Russia from his predecessors and perhaps of his own ability to bring about that return to real world-power status, as opposed to being a shadow world power, which Russia is now. I think that in a way Mr. Putin could do us all a great service by making rather threatening speeches about how important Russia is going to be. It might just give that impetus back to the enlargement process, so you wouldn't have to wait another 13 years. Thirteen years, by the way, pessimists think is when Britain will join the euro.

I must say a quick word about widening and deepening. I think widening, originally, was a great objective of Mrs. Thatcher. She had fond words about Prague, Warsaw and other parts of Europe and she saw this as a way of having a much more loosely associated consort of European states. Since then it has become clear that an enlarged Europe cannot work without more majority voting. The dangers of one small country being able to hold up the whole process are too great. So the British now have to agree to deepening if they want widening, and history shows that widening and deepening have in fact gone hand in hand. We [the EU] started with six countries, much less integrated than the 15 countries now are, and I think the two will continue hand in hand.

I think the real political problem with enlargement is that it is going to cost money, and the existing 15 countries are becoming more and more money conscious. They can agree on a budget that has some modest redistribution within the 15, but if it is a question of finding more money for the accession countries, then every country, including Spain, will become a net contributor to the budget and the only net beneficiaries will be the Central and Eastern European countries. I think that requires a degree of altruism, which is not evidenced in the present public opinion polls about enlargement in the Western countries. Therefore, I think we shouldn't underestimate the difficulties, nor should we underestimate the importance of actually proceeding with enlargement for political, foreign policy, defense, and security reasons.

NORBERT WALTER: I think if we do proper analysis, we do not need altruism. We just need enlightened self-interest as a guide to be positive about enlargement. I think we have seen that the enlargement to the south has helped those countries that were willing to allow funds to go there, and the same will happen again. If we consider that our taxpayers are not willing to pay at the present burden, we should come up with more imaginative ideas like privatization of infrastructure, rather than channeling more funds from taxpayers' coffers into roads, highways or railways further east.

ROBERT MUNDELL: Well I was feeling very discouraged until the last two speakers, because I detected a note of euro-pessimism, and it is disturbing coming to the extent it does within Eastern Europe itself. I was recently on a trip to Warsaw and Moscow and Kiev and so on, and in Poland we talked about the euro. Recent polls showed at one point that 80 percent of the Poles were in favor of joining the EU. Recently that had gone down to something like 35 percent, an astonishingly low number. I talked about this with the president of Poland who recognized that this was a very disturbing element. His own view is that Poland has to move as quickly as possible to enter the EMU. Recently, there were headlines in the [International] *Herald Tribune* that he had made a statement that Western Europe should not be selfish and impede or delay the accession of the Eastern countries. I think if this pessimism about Europe starts to pervade the countries in Central and Eastern Europe, it will be self-fulfilling. There are too many forces in Western Europe that are unwilling to pay the costs that are needed to make the restructuring changes. This may put the whole process off for another seven or eight years that I think is much too long. It may be that after seven years the option will not be open anymore. Who knows what is going to happen on the geopolitical front?

This is like the unification of Germany and the freedom that countries took on when the Soviet Union was collapsing. It was a wonderful opportunity to leap at the chance to do things when the opening was there, and not worry too much about the costs, because in the long run the costs will be overcome by the benefits. I think when Václav Klaus talks about the natural rate of inflation in transition countries, whatever that means, being higher there than in the other countries, I suppose you can make an argument that with any kind of restructuring that is going to go on, a little bit of inflation helps rather than hurts. However, I do not think that you should pay too much attention to this argument, because the costs of that may be much higher. I think the gains that a country gets from zeroing in on an efficient monetary system for the whole economy, for the monetary and fiscal discipline that it provides, and the direction of investment is vastly more important than any little extra benefit that higher inflation provides. I think that the best approach for all the Central and Eastern European countries that are planning to accede would be to move as quickly as possible, as quickly as their budgets permit, to a fixed exchange rate relationship tailored to their own economies, including currency board arrangements that would give them a taste of what monetary union would really be like.

I think that one big benefit that all those countries would get would be a drastic reduction of interest rates. Instead of having interest rates of 10 percent or 20 percent, they would get an interest rate of 5 percent. The impact of that in helping out with the private market restructuring that needs to take place, as well as the easing of the burden on the public debt, would be vastly greater than the costs.

VÁCLAV KLAUS: Just a terminological dispute. I would prefer instead of using the terms "euro-pessimism" and "euro-optimism," which are journalistic expressions, I always prefer to talk about "euro-realism" and "euro-naïvism." That is my opinion.

RICHARD COOPER: I just want to comment on Bob's last point about an interest rate reduction. We actually have an experiment with that – it is called Argentina. It has been pegged to the US dollar for nine years now, going on ten. The reduction of interest rates has been much less than was forecast by people like Bob at the time. So this is a possibility, but it is not a sure thing.

ROBERT MUNDELL: There are different types of fixed exchange rate systems. Argentina does not have a currency board; it has a currency board-like system. Argentina could very easily, throughout the period, have kept interest rates down had they also not simply fixed the spot peso rate to the dollar at one to one, but had fixed the forward peso rate to the dollar at one to one. Throughout this whole period they would have saved a huge amount of money for the budget and for the country by having very low interest rates, which would have been close to the American level. In any case, because of the EU element, this is different.

Argentina is not politically linked to the US, the country to which it is pegging. But the accession countries are going to be linked politically to the EU countries, and I think that here there is an element that Europe itself can learn from the French as the French treasury guaranteed the 13 CFA currencies in Africa. That guarantee is something the ECB will be able to utilize if it wants to support interest rates that will fall.

RICHARD COOPER: That's a completely different proposition than the one you first made. To get a guarantee from Europeans of these things is a different proposition from their linking their currencies to Europe.

ROBERT MUNDELL: Well, that depends. Let's say Slovenia decides to have a currency board fixed to the euro and it makes it credible and it cooperates and has this arrangement with ECB. Even without the guarantee, if everything in that country is credible, I have no doubt that interest rates in Slovenia will get down to below 6 percent.

RICHARD COOPER: Such experience as we have with this kind of claim does not support that. That's wishful thinking.

ROBERT MUNDELL: But you're talking about Argentina.

RICHARD COOPER: And Estonia and Italy until the euro was actually at hand.

ROBERT MUNDELL: Italy never had a currency board. I thought they should have moved toward that and they would have gotten their interest rates down. Had they done it, had they fixed the lira to the DM at a thousand to the DM, and then lopped off three zeroes, it would have been a very credible kind of arrangement. Had they introduced, which was my proposal, a law in government that would take a two-thirds majority of both parts of the Italian parliament in order to change the exchange, I am absolutely certain interest rates would have been brought down.

RICHARD COOPER: Especially if they would have gotten a guarantee from the German government, I agree with you. Let me make two other points on the demand by the rest of the world for the euro. This will have exchange rate consequences, and this is a source of outward pressure on the exchange rate unrelated to internal economic developments in Europe or in Europe's trading partners. The first point is, will Europe be comfortable with the upward pressure on its exchange rates coming from desire around the world to hold financial instruments in euros.

Second point: there are a lot of dollars held around the world today. One can at least imagine the possibility, say, ten years from now, in which hundreds of billions of dollars' worth of euros are held by central banks, monetary authorities, and private parties. Through processes that we don't have to specify, sentiment changes between the euro and the dollar, one can imagine a variety of circumstances under which one would observe let's call them lurches, in portfolios between dollars and euros, the immediate pressure of which will be taken on the exchange rates. It is not inconceivable to imagine changes in the euro–dollar rate of 10 percent in a week. We have actually seen that in the case of the Japanese yen. So my question to you all is, under those circumstances, would Europe be comfortable with a laissez-faire attitude toward the exchange rate? Would the council of ministers want to give orientations [i.e. directions for exchange rate changes], and if it were to give orientations, what would the orientations be?

CHRISTOPHER JOHNSON: I want to start off this discussion by reminding people where we are now. The position is, broadly, that the euro is much more important vis-à-vis the dollar in the private sector than it is in the official reserve sector. Looking at figures that are about a year old gives us an idea of magnitude. If we look at international (cross-border) credit, then domestic credit, there is a huge amount in the US, relative to Europe. The euro accounts for 20 percent of world international bank loans, and the dollar accounts for 35 percent. If Britain and other countries were to join, that figure would go up to about 23 percent, so there is a gap there, but not a huge one. There is a bigger gap in the bond markets. The euro again accounts for about 20 percent of international bonds and the dollar about 48 percent, but the catch up in the bond market has begun within the last year.

RICHARD COOPER: Just so I'm clear, you are talking about outstanding stocks?

CHRISTOPHER JOHNSON: Yes, outstanding stocks at the end of 1998. What I am saying is that I do not think there is going to be a huge move out of dollars into euros. We are talking about relative rates of increase in the different stocks. I think the hypothesis would be that the share of the euro is going to increase gradually at the expense of the share in the dollar. Both are going to rise in importance, and the role of the yen is relatively small now, it is only 10 percent of world international bank loans and about 15 percent of bonds.

Another dimension we can look at is the currency of invoicing and you've got what you might call the rate of internationalization: how much more is a currency used in world trade than the share of that country in world exports? We find the US at 16 percent of world exports, the dollar at 45 percent of all trade invoicing, so it has a ratio of three, three times as important as the US exports would suggest. For the euro, or euro constituent currencies, we are looking at 20 percent of world exports, and 28 percent of world invoicing, so that is a 1.4 ratio. The euro is used outside euro-land for exports, but not nearly as much as the dollar. Of course, the importance is that when a currency starts being more widely used for invoicing, the market using it becomes more liquid, margins become finer and there is an advantage to users of that currency given the size of the market.

If we look at official reserves, which are much smaller in quantity than the private use of currencies, the dollar still accounts for 57 percent and the euro only 15 percent, and gold is about 14 percent at current values. The euro still has a long way to go before it catches up to the dollar in reserves. I think one needs to dismiss as fantasy a lot of the talk about how suddenly overnight the euro has become as important as the dollar. It will take quite a long time, and financial markets have to develop, make themselves more attractive, cheaper to use, and the advantage of size, which the dollar has, is that it is cheaper to use now, and therefore the euro has got a long way to go to cut down the barriers to usage and make itself as attractive to use as the dollar in international finance.

MANFRED NEUMANN: May I say something about the numbers, because I have recently looked at the BIS [Bank of International Settlements] statistics and we have numbers from September 1999. We have stock data and we have flow data. The stock data is as follows: if you take together international bonds and money market instruments, where money market instruments are a small market compared to international bonds, then the stocks are about 48 percent for the dollar, 28 percent for the euro, and the Japanese yen is at 11 percent or 12 percent. If you look at the flows just to see what happened over the first three quarters of 1999, then you find the following: the Japanese yen lost during those three quarters, the dollar gained, but the euro gained more, in absolute percentage terms, but it is not impressive, so we really have to wait.

CHRISTOPHER JOHNSON: I think that is quite consistent with my figures, but there is a difference in classification. There are quite a lot of domestic bonds, which are aimed chiefly at foreign investors. If you include those in the figures, you get a bigger share for the euro.

PAUL FABRA: Richard [Cooper], I'll just come back to what you just said that we could envisage a moment when the weekly fluctuation between the dollar and the euro could attain 10 percent or so. Afterwards you asked whether the euro-zone would be happy with that, and I personally would not envisage them to intervene. That is very important because this means that in your view the introduction of the euro is very unlikely to change, in the visible future, the basic stance of the US, which is not to intervene in foreign exchange markets except in a few circumstances. So you think the fact that there are two important possible currencies in the world will not change that?

RICHARD COOPER: I did not mean to express any views. I meant to pose a question. To be concrete, for the same reasons that Niels [Thygesen] gave with respect to a relatively relaxed attitude by Europe during the course of 1999 on the depreciation of the euro against the dollar (namely that it provided some economic stimulus in a period in which economic stimulus was welcome). I have to say that the US, and I now speak about the system as whole, not academic economists, is just as mercantilist in its attitudes as Europe is. I can imagine rates of change that will produce headlines, but if it is a weakening of the dollar, there are a lot of folks who would welcome that. Consider a concrete experiment: yesterday the possibility was mentioned that the leading oil producing countries might denominate oil in euros at some point in the future. If that were so, anyone paying for oil will accumulate euros prior to the big payment periods as they accumulate dollars now. The exporters will presumably hold a much higher ratio of euros in their reserves and a lower ratio of dollars. If that change were to occur rapidly, I can imagine quite dramatic change in the world's portfolio holdings and a corresponding impact on exchange rates. One can ask about a number of such possibilities. I do not forecast any of them, but just as possibilities, one can ask how the system as a whole would react. Certainly under some circumstances the Americans would become very concerned if, for example, it were associated with a major disturbance in domestic US markets. This would engage the financial officials directly, so one has to be somewhat more precise. I was really posing the issue for the Europeans since most of the participants around the table are European.

ROBERT PRINGLE: I thought the group might be interested in the summary of a survey that my magazine, *Central Banking*, carried out of central banks around the world last year. This occurred a few months after the beginning of the euro. One hundred central banks replied to the survey about reserve policies, and of these, a great majority thought that it would be a number of years before the euro became what we call a fully-fledged international reserve currency. The reasons for this were quite interesting. The first was the lack of a unified capital market in Europe and the kind of nitty-gritty thing that Alexandre Lamfalussy talked about. The second and third most important reasons were lack of political union and divergent fiscal policies in the euro area. These are the views of central bank reserve managers around the world. The possibility of divergent fiscal policies inside Europe were obviously weighed quite heavily with these central banks when they thought about diversifying their reserves away from the dollar to the euro. Having said that, the majority also said that they planned actually to move some of their reserves to euros in the next period. Moreover, the vast majority believed that within ten years, the euro markets would be as deep and liquid as those in the US. This was essentially a short to medium term worry, except for the problem of divergent fiscal policies, which, obviously given the enlargement discussion we had earlier on, has the possibility of being made worse after the enlargement. The scenario of a quick rush of central bank holdings from the dollar to the euro is not very realistic.

MANFRED NEUMANN: There is a long article in the monthly [August, 1999] report of the ECB dealing with various aspects of the euro becoming an international currency. It also looks at some numbers. The important thing is that at the end of the article, the bank has a statement implying that they do know it creates complications for internal policy if the euro becomes an international currency, but they are prepared for this. This means that they would like to see the euro become an international currency. Why? I think because they think about the long-run seigniorage issue. If you think in political-economic terms, then you could say that it also gives you more power as a central bank.

The other thing I wanted to say is something about general exchange rate orientations. At the start of 1999, the ECB made statements about the general understanding of how to run monetary policy. In this respect, they also touched on general exchange rate orientations. My understanding is, and I would support them in this view, that they do not want to see an exchange rate orientation because this could be interpreted by the European public as an attempt by the European governments to take away a little bit of independence from the bank. Although the governments have the right to do this according to the Maastricht Treaty, nevertheless, a *de facto* independence is very important. If you think these situations are true, then this means the ECB has to avoid a situation where the governments would be tempted to do this. This means that in the case of a larger exchange rate movement towards appreciation, they will have to do some leaning against the wind, so that the [EU countries'] governments are happy.

ALEXANDRE LAMFALUSSY: I would like to make two remarks. One concerns the constitutional question about who determines exchange rate policy for the euro area. Unfortunately, I haven't got the treaty text here, but if I quote by memory I do not think I will be wrong on the substance, but I may be wrong on the words. It is the council (i.e. the governments) that decides on the general exchange rate policy orientation. They do so either on the recommendation of the ECB, or on the recommendation of the Commission, after having heard the view of the ECB. In the treaty in at least two different places, it is said very clearly that these policies cannot be in conflict with the duty of the ECB to preserve price stability. One must think about what the tools are of carrying out an exchange rate policy. They are basically two: intervention and interest rate policy, and both have monetary policy consequences. There is a practical obligation to agree between the governments and the central bank. There is no way out.

Let me try to respond to your question and think five or ten years ahead. Let us assume that we do have a use for the euro in international portfolios, both central bank and private portfolios, comparable in size to those of the dollar. A sort of bipolar system. What could happen in that situation? If I am optimistic, which I am not naturally, I would say that this is a situation where we might have a certain balance of interests between the US and the euro area in the stabilization of the euro–dollar rate that we do not have at present. On the one hand, the degree of openness between the two areas will be approximately similar, and therefore the inflationary impact can be similar in both cases if there is depreciation. On the other hand, expectations of exchange rate changes may trigger capital flows and portfolio readjustments and therefore create domestic problems. One of the reasons why, before the euro area, countries could not really afford to practice benign neglect of the exchange rate was that it triggered capital outflows. If that sort of situation arises for the US, we may have a more balanced interest to try to stabilize. Whether that can be successful or not is a consideration. I just do not believe that today one can stabilize the dollar–euro rate if the stabilization is pursued only by one of the two parties. I think this is not credible in that the market would not believe that it would have an effect, and therefore it is very important that the stabilization effort comes from both sides. In the sense of joint intervention agreements and/or agreed adjustment of interest rates, I am not very optimistic about the feasibility of this sort of agreement, but it is conceivable that with a better balance of interests, it could happen.

NORBERT WALTER: I would caution against being carried away with the stock data and rather look into what may be important factors that change the composition of reserves. I would again point to a number of issues that we already have addressed: that a number of countries, certainly in Europe and around Europe, will be anchoring their exchange rate policies to the euro. This obviously has a bearing for their composition of reserves. If you look into the debate in Asia, they perfectly understand that the yen is not the solution for everything and that the dollar has not been a good solution either, so there is more willingness and openness to address the issue of a different approach towards their exchange rate regime and their reserves.

Secondly, intra-European trade flows are accelerating and this should be an important factor for reserves. There is another issue that I wanted to point to. With the surplus in the government balances in the United States we have a reduction in the supply of government bonds. The world's institutional investors are not capable and/or willing to consider [US] corporate bonds as a full substitute for government bonds. Under such circumstances, European [government] bonds are an attractive alternative and this should have an implication for the euro as well.

CHRISTOPHER JOHNSON: If the Growth and Stability Pact is adhered to, there will not be any more euro government bonds issued either.

NORBERT WALTER: In relative terms, certainly, the supply of government bonds will change in favor of the Europeans.

ROBERT BARTLEY: On the issue of benign neglect, I sympathize with the widespread European feeling that there is very little advantage if the ECB abandons benign neglect in the exchange rate unless the Fed does as well. So I thought I would give you a little political reading of the likelihood of change in Federal Reserve policy. It is a very small minority of Americans who would advocate the abandonment of benign neglect at this moment. I think I can count about three of them, and they are all in this room. Now its not exactly hopeless because Bob [Mundell] and I were alone together on tax policy in the late 1970s and we did not have the support of anyone like Paul Volcker at that point. The most likely change in Fed policy would come from a change of administration. The chief economic advisor to [Governor and Presidential candidate George W.] Bush is [Federal Reserve Board Governor, 1991–97] Larry Lindsey. Lindsey is wonderful on fiscal policy but on monetary policy, he is very conventional. Paul [Volcker], you might work on him a little bit if you can.

In all of this, I am reminded of some of the discussions I have also participated in regarding national security policy over this same period in which we also saw some big reversals in US policy and thinking. The great persuader is always *events*. So I think if we were going to have a change in benign neglect on the part of the Federal Reserve, it would have to be because of some event, or as one of my national security people said, we need to fall off a medium-sized cliff.

NICOLAS KRUL: I have three short remarks. The first one is about your mention of a 10 percent eventuality. This should not be forgotten, because it so happened last February 28th or 29th, the euro declined by 3.5 percent in one day, because of one single transaction. These things happen and they could repeat themselves.

The second point is that I am convinced that over time, international portfolios will include a much bigger share of the euro. This is unavoidable in terms of risk diversification for the international investment community. At the same time, I am not worried about sharp changes in that process, because international investors respond gradually.

The third remark is that the direction of international capital markets could improve exchange rate management; Alexandre Lamfalussy mentioned this. I think this is really an important point and I share the belief that this might be an opening to future exchange rate management because it is not only a matter of an efficient allocation of international capital, but also because I think that given the growth in US external liabilities, it will become an essential concern for American policymakers. The ECB and the Japanese will share this concern. On the whole, this is a point that might be usefully developed over time by the academic community.

RICHARD COOPER: I need some help from Alexandre [Lamfalussy] and from the others. My understanding is that the Maastricht Treaty enjoins the ECB to achieve price stability. Our preoccupation over the last 40 years or more has been with inflation. A rapid appreciation of the euro does not threaten price stability in that sense. So how would the ECB justify an intervention in the event of a major US current account deficit that, for example, led the investment community around the world to invest less in the US? What would be the rationale in the institutional framework that we now have for ECB intervention under those circumstances?

ALEXANDRE LAMFALUSSY: I think the answer is quite simple. The primary objective of the ECB, given by the treaty, is to preserve price stability. But it is also written very clearly that without prejudice to the pursuit of that objective, the ECB is supposed to support general government policies. It then refers back to what those policies are. The treaty says that those policies include the objective of sustainable growth and a high level of employment.

RICHARD COOPER: We heard from Manfred [Neumann] that the ECB is resistant to the idea of guidelines from the governments, so is the ECB, without guidelines, supposed to intuit what government policies are by reading the newspapers?

ALEXANDRE LAMFALUSSY: If the ECB did not do that, it would not have lowered its interest rate sometime ago. According to the mandate, they have to support general economic policies, and the general economic policies of that time were attempting to accelerate growth in Europe.

ROBERT SKILDELSKY: I just wanted to take up a point that Richard Cooper made about benign neglect. Professor Lamfalussy also had some very interesting thoughts on that by way of historical analogy. I think one of the lessons that came out of the 1930s was that currency exchange rate changes were a two-way affair, in other words, there has to be acquiescence by one country "A" to a change in the value of currency in country "B." The danger is that you do get into competitive currency wars.

In the 1930s there were two major reserve currencies: the dollar and [British pound] sterling. In 1931, sterling was devalued against gold, its value therefore went down against the dollar, and 20 countries or so joined sterling in a joint float. The Americans did not acquiesce in the devaluation of sterling. In 1933 they followed monetary policies that deliberately brought the value of the dollar down, so that by 1933 the rate of exchange between the two currencies was exactly the same as in 1930.

Bob Bartley says that there are only three people today [in the US] who believe in anything other than a policy of benign neglect. In fact, in 1933 there were only three people who believed anything other than that. By 1936 they had reached an agreement, because the costs of a currency war seemed to be too great. I would say that there are costs today with a policy of benign neglect between the two major currencies. There are costs to an open trading system, because if you have mercantilist monetary policies, they tend to have an impact on your trade policies.

Secondly, there are political costs. It sours relations between the two main blocks. I would say that over time, and it may not be such a long time, the costs of continuing with a policy of benign neglect, and what Richard [Cooper] called mercantilist policies, will actually be considered too great. How the rules of adjustment will be worked out is unknown and is a problem of great interest. I think the continuation of the present system is going to be seen to impose severe costs and I think it will not go on for very much longer.

ROBERT MUNDELL: My criticism refers to the first part of Robert's [Skidelsky] statement, the second part I agree with. It is this issue of beggar-thy-neighbor policies (or currency competition). This was the big bug-a-bear of the 1930s that Joan Robinson [1903–83] wrote about and got spread throughout the economics literature. I do not agree with it at all. I think that there is a factor in it that is missing. The currency competition in the 1930s, not necessarily today, but in the 1930s, was a very good thing, because countries were on a version of the gold standard. The big problem in the 1930s was that countries went back to the gold standard at prices that undervalued gold by about 40 percent. I talked about that yesterday. This is what brought on the Wall Street crash and the great deflation – there was a 30 percent deflation of major currencies over that period. Britain opted out of it and I think Britain not only did the right thing, but also should have done so earlier. America also should have opted out very quickly because the price of gold in terms of dollars would have gone up three years before the United States devalued the dollar and raised the price of gold from its former official price of \$20.67 to \$35. This was a movement in the right direction. If we would have had more currency competition in the 1930s, we would have had less deflation and we would not have had the Great Depression, and we probably would not have had World War II.

ENZO GRILLI: I would like to comment on the second point of Professor Skidelsky's historical analogy and the fears that he expressed regarding the positive correlation between benign neglect and mercantilist trade policies. Benign neglect is undefined. If one looks at the volatility of exchange rates over the period of 1973–98, one observes that volatility has not increased. Volatility is almost exactly the same in the first of half of the period and the second half of the period. You do not even need to do statistical tests. Volatility is not exploding.

Secondly, if you look at the trends, and they are much more noticeable on the Japanese–dollar relations than on the euro–dollar relations, there are some trends, but they are not terribly uniform. They lack a unifying direction. Given that that's my notion of benign neglect in terms of consequences, one has to ask oneself, what are the consequences of that on trade flows? The consequences of that on trade flows are not terribly damaging. They did not prevent a healthy expansion of world trade during this period.

Another question is what are the effects on trade policies? It is a very important question. I've been very concerned about that through the 1970s, 1980s and 1990s. There is a relationship between cycles in the exchange rates and trade policies in the direction that you indicate and that I myself fear. They are not very strong cycles because they get reflected through non-tariff [barriers to trade] policies. To my surprise, those mercantilist effects or variability of cycles in exchange rates have not been very large.

ROBERT SKIDELSKY: On the point made just now, I was really positing a new situation that had arisen since the creation of the euro. We have only had one year's experience of that. For the first time we have two potentially mercantilist blocks. We now have an aggregation of monetary power in one of them which is on a completely different scale to anything we have seen since 1973. So it was really in that context that I was expressing my worries.

On the point made by Professor Mundell, I was not questioning whether Britain was right to opt out of the gold standard in 1931, I was simply making the point that America did not acquiesce. I do not believe that sterling was overvalued at the time. It thought it was correctly valued and therefore brought back the value of the dollar to what I believed was the correct one, which was five dollars to one pound, where it stayed until the Americans did finally acquiesce in 1936–37 to further sterling depreciation. But, it had to be done by agreement. During that period, we also know that Britain formed the Imperial Preference System [the British trading system that led to the General Agreement on Trade and Tariffs], and you did get a close correlation between the sterling area and imperial preference system; they were not identical, but people did talk about two mercantilist blocks, and it enormously soured the relations between the British Empire and the United States in the 1930s. They had a currency and trade war, and made the creation of a united front against fascism extremely difficult. The 1936 monetary agreement and 1938 trade agreement were the beginning of an adjustment of the relations between the two blocks. I am suggesting that the benefits of agreements on these matters will be more obvious to the two areas than the costs of non-agreement or benign neglect.

ROBERT MUNDELL: Maybe when you say that the United States did not acquiesce there is a time period involved in this. I think the United States acquiesced in September 1931, when [the value of] sterling floated downward. There was no devaluation, but the sterling was allowed to devalue and it went down substantially against the dollar. The US acquiesced in that it did not change its policy with respect to gold; in fact it tripled interest rates and became more rigidly on the gold standard than before, dragging the United States deeper into the depression. I agree with you [that the US acquiesced] after the devaluation of the dollar when the US floated in 1933. This was a very acrimonious issue from 1933 to 1935 when Americans did not want sterling to be devalued against the dollar. So I am merely quibbling about your prior statement that initially there was acquiescence. The newly installed [Franklin D.] Roosevelt administration didn't acquiesce in devaluation. It seems too bad to me that the US did acquiesce in 1931, because if they had floated in 1931, instead of tightening money and aggravating the depression, it would have been much better for the US and the rest of the world.

MASSIMILIANO MARZO: I have a brief remark on the role of the euro as an international currency. I think that trade flows are important in improving the role of the euro as a vehicle currency. One important thing is the role of the euro for exchange in international financial markets. In this respect, there are two perspectives. First, consider the international equity markets and international fixed income securities. With respect to fixed income securities, as we have already heard, the situation in Europe is very good because we recently converted all internal debt into euro-denominated debt. The effects are already evident in the government bond markets where spreads have narrowed and we have more liquid benchmark issues. The government is shifting to fewer larger issues because this improves liquidity in the market. I expect that European denominated government bonds will become much more important in the future. This is crucial in defining the euro as an international currency since government bonds serve as collateral for open market operations in foreign exchange markets.

Something else has to be done in equity markets. The recent merger of the stock market in Europe [the stock markets of Paris, Brussels, and Amsterdam merged in 2000] is a first step towards more integration. What is going to happen to the southern European stock markets? I am particularly concerned about Italy and Spain. [Another merger] would improve integration of stock markets in Europe. If this does not occur in the near future, then I suspect that the euro cannot become an important international currency. Of course, this does not eliminate the asymmetric information of international investors. If the euro becomes a true competitor to the US dollar, then the next question is: how will the competition for international seigniorage be solved?

Should we expect higher volatility of the exchange rate after these steps are taken?

MANFRED NEUMANN: Yesterday I started to discuss benign neglect; I did not mean that one should never intervene. A policy of benign neglect simply means that you do not make the exchange rate the focal point of your policy. This does not imply that if there is a large change you will not do anything, but it certainly means that you will not enter into an official exchange rate arrangement.

I would like to come back to the second objective of the ECB that was copied from the Bundesbank law. In an international context, there is a general economic policy formulated by the government and so the central bank will to some extent support this. In the context of the euro-area that is difficult. First of all, there is no general economic policy. I know there is a catalogue of objectives written into the treaty, but that does not make a policy. An economic policy that the ECB would take into account requires coordination of economic policies in the euro-area that we have yet to observe. There are stipulations in the treaty for doing this, but they do not *require* action, so it is unlikely that much will occur. It seems to me that this second objective really does not play a role.

RICHARD COOPER: I think the first of Manfred's two points is the most important. The worst thing that can happen in both academic and policy dialogues is that people use the same terms with different meanings so non-conversations are taking place even though people seem to be talking. I think I am right in saying that benign neglect, and for those who do not like it, they call it "malign" neglect in the US, actually means staying out of the foreign exchange market most of the time. We had an Undersecretary of the Treasury in the first Reagan administration [1981–84] named Barry Sprinkle, and when he was pressed on this issue he said if there is an attempted assassination and a market disturbance it does not absolutely exclude market intervention, but [intervention] will be a rare event. As I heard Manfred, he said [intervention] is not that rare an event, but that there is not a policy target for the exchange rate.

MANFRED NEUMANN: I am absolutely with you.

RICHARD COOPER: So you are with Barry Sprinkle on this. Okay, it is useful to have that clarification.

PAUL VOLCKER: I was particularly startled to hear if there is no trend in volatility [in the last 25 years] then the situation was acceptable. Let me review the record of the period during which there has been no change in volatility. Beginning in 1973 when floating began, the dollar declined by 25 percent in a year. A couple of years later [the dollar was back to its original value]. By 1978 it had reached a crisis point provoking, in this great country of benign neglect, a fierce defense of the dollar policy with the full armory of massive intervention, including borrowing foreign currencies and raising the discount rate by 1 percent. Six years later the dollar was 80 percent higher, only to come down again a few years later. In the 1990s we have it going up and down by 60 percent or 70 percent against the yen over the course of a few years. That may not be a statistically [significant] change in volatility, but I would suggest it is a problem.

All I heard in the 1970s from [1976 Nobel Laureate and Chicago economist] Milton Friedman and others, was just wait until things settle down, we've got to have a learning period, and we expect volatility in an inflationary world economy. We have now had 28 years to learn, and we do not have an inflationary world economy. We have price levels in Japan, the United States and Europe for some years being almost the same in terms of trend and [exchange rate] volatility has not decreased. I would suggest, from all I heard this morning except for three people, that there is no future prospect that volatility will decrease between the two major currencies. Neither of them cares; both of them have a big internal market. Financial markets are becoming more fluid; it is easier and easier to move the money. I assure you that money will move if private operators think that the authorities do not care and are not going to do anything about it.

What about the weighted average exchange rate? I consider myself an expert in this area since I made up the thing when we were devaluing the dollar and wanted to show the Europeans how little it was being devalued, so we made up a weighted average exchange rate. When the dollar depreciates by 20 percent against the yen and appreciates by 20 percent against the euro, the weighted average changes very little. It disguises the real volatility in the market and does not tell you anything useful. You know the famous analogy, I feel comfortable when I have my foot in ice water and my head under a hot shower, so the average is okay. The problem is that under present circumstances there is no indication that volatility is decreasing. What really puzzles me is the enormous political energy that has been expended in recent years to reduce and eliminate tariffs, through trade negotiations in a period when there is a lot of political resistance, yet there is great, I will use the term benign neglect, about exchange rate volatility. The inference of this is that [exchange rate volatility] has nothing to do with trade and investment. I just find that a striking refutation of price theory [differentials in price]. A lot of other things are supporting an increase in international trade, but certainly they take different and presumably less efficient channels than reasonable [exchange rate] stability. How can it not affect trade?

All of the discussions this morning were concerned with the development of a euro block. I think that is perfectly natural. I think that one more Latin American financial crisis, which is readily predictable within the course of ten years or so, will bring a dollar block in the Western Hemisphere. There is a much more difficult situation in Asia because, as many people have mentioned, the yen cannot play the same role since trade is much more diversified. I see the prospect of two blocks with a lot of volatility between them and a kind of mess in Asia because there is no anchor [currency]. I do not know whether this will lead to economic warfare, but it is not a world I particularly like and I think it has some dangers in it. It seems to me that the real question we ought to be grappling with is not whether this is good, since it cannot be good, but whether there are practical ways of dealing with it. Can we be successful in trying to deal with it?

A major argument I hear all the time is that one cannot do anything to stabilize [exchange rates] because the market is too big and too strong. I do not really believe that. It constantly mystifies me how there can be a preoccupation in the US and around the world as to whether the Federal Reserve will or will not change interest rates by one-quarter of 1 percent in the next three months. That is debated endlessly with all kinds of influences on financial markets. The market is so sensitive to the kind of interest rate change that I used to think was too small to bother with. Yet somehow these authorities with all this influence have no influence on the exchange rate even though it is going to disrupt their internal price stability. Exchange rates are two-sided; it cannot disrupt both sides' internal price stability at the same time, sometimes it helps, sometimes it does not help. I would suggest to you that in a world with the objective of price stability broadly accepted and successfully implemented, the trend of prices is not going to be upset by normal intervention in the [foreign] exchange markets. One side of the equation or the other is bound to help and not hurt, even in that limited context.

Given that all of the above may be true, the question remains: can we in fact affect the [foreign exchange] market? Judgments differ on this. I would certainly agree that it takes agreement on both sides. There has to be some kind of a balanced or agreed approach. It is going to at least involve the threat of an adjustment in monetary policy as well as intervention. To have a credible threat requires that [unilateral] policy changes occasionally occur. The game is whether you can develop a sense of "equilibrating" speculation (to go back to those old terms), instead of "dis-equilibrating" speculation, which pushes one further away. I think we have our bellies full of "dis-equilibrating" speculation where people have made money, and continue to make money by going with the trend. I think you have to change that atmosphere, change that mood, and I think it is possible to do it.

MAX CORDEN: A quick question for Paul. I have heard it said by Japanese economists that in the middle or late 1980s, pressure was put on Japan to prevent further depreciation of the dollar, and that led to monetary expansion in Japan causing their big bubble. The basic argument is that an attempt to stabilize exchange rates did have an adverse domestic effect in Japan, and I would like your opinion on that.

PAUL VOLCKER: It is hard for me to reconstruct all that. The bottom line is that I do not think that [monetary policy] was the whole cause of the problems in Japan. It was a bad policy mistake, however. I cannot even remember if that is when the dollar was depreciating.

RICHARD COOPER: The market pressures on the dollar were allegedly downward and there was this intervention by Japan.

PAUL VOLCKER: But that was very late in the day for the Japanese bubble.

If I can just make one comment on that period, I would like to say that one of my great regrets is that in 1987, when there was great pressure on the dollar, we should have tightened the money [supply] faster than we did and we should have intervened [in the currency markets]. After the Louvre Accord, we should have been doing it. The Louvre Accord was much too narrow and precise in my view, but it was in the right direction. We should have had a more forceful domestic policy that would have saved us a lot of agony if we would have tightened up sooner than we did, partly because of exchange rate uncertainty.

ALEXANDRE LAMFALUSSY: I just looked up the facts. Between the spring of 1985 and early spring 1988, both the yen and the D-mark appreciated against the dollar by 100 percent, both in nominal and real terms. The [devaluation] between 1985 and 1988 more than wiped out the appreciation of the dollar between 1980 and 1985. One personal note: in late 1987, when the dollar was at the lowest point, I could not pay my hotel bill in London with dollars because they were not accepted. This is not prehistory, it was twelve years ago.

EMIL CLAASSEN: The intervention [in the late 1980s] was so huge that world reserves doubled in eighteen months.

PAUL ZAK: I want to make a quick clarifying point on what Paul Volcker said. There is evidence that the Fed does affect the foreign exchange markets. If you look at the Fed's earnings, you see that since they have been intervening in the foreign exchange markets they have made money almost every year, which means they must be leading the market. So people observe the Fed's signals and seem to follow them. The data seems to suggest that the Fed does affect the markets in terms of direction.

ROBERT MUNDELL: I would like to discuss the volatility of exchange rates, and I agree with Paul [Volcker] on this completely. There are great advantages to capital market integration from fixed exchange rates and great disturbances to capital market integration by volatile exchange rates. Volatility creates inefficiencies in financial markets, and volatility is completely unnecessary. I would like to see the absence of volatility. The best way I can put this is by starting with the endgame. Supposing we decided that Japan, the US and Europe had licked inflation and they were convergent in that sense. Then suppose they did what the EU 11 did and they form a G3 block with a common currency, a single currency union of these three areas. In that union there will be an equalization of interest rates. This would be close to, in some sense, an ideal system. One would have to have an integration of policy decisions to expand, just as the EU 11 does, and a division of the seigniorage and in ways that are pretty obvious. If you started with that system and then you had integration of the 60 percent of the world economy that this represents, who would ever think to want to break up capital markets in countries around the world by introducing three separate currencies? If you start with a unified system that produces stability of price levels according to a common index of prices, who would ever want to move to a system such as we have now, with the volatility and all the costs and all the political bitterness associated with it? There is, of course, the political problem of how you get to monetary union and whether you would want to have a single currency monetary union, or a three currency monetary union. I would also like to emphasize a point that Paul made, that we shouldn't be talking about whether the volatility is good or bad, it is obviously bad, every economist knows it is bad, the question is how do we eliminate it and what are the necessary political steps.

HERBERT GIERSCH: I wanted to come in when I heard "currency war." I was reminded that there was ruinous currency competition in the 1930s. This was another way of raising the price of gold. It could have been done by agreement, but it was done by competition.

I also wanted to underline a more positive aspect to which Robert Skidelsky referred last night. [Skildelsky] said that a more credible sanction against inflation-prone governments than commitment to an exchange rate target is international financial flows leaving countries that do not deserve the confidence that has been given to them. Competition for internationally mobile capital is a substitute for trade wars. This has led to a hardening of the system. Those who deviate from people's expectations are being punished by volatility or a currency crisis. Volatility, however, has a high cost. What is required is a judgment of the medium and long-run parity [of exchange rates], but who has this knowledge? This is close to [1974 Nobel Laureate Friedrich] Hayek's notion of the pretense of knowledge – that we behave as if we have knowledge of the future and can fix rates so to exclude volatility.

Competition is moving us to a system that is more stable than it used to be because countries have learned to avoid situations where mobile capital is leaving the currency area. There is a tendency to be loyal to your promises, not to deviate from the expectations that you have created. There is a possibility of calling this competition a trade war, but you also can say this is a natural rivalry that takes place in human life. This is a substitute for an agreement that would fix [exchange rates] to the price of gold. Since life is unpredictable, there has to be some volatility.

The markets are more future-oriented under the influence of declining communication costs than in the past. So expectations play a greater role than they did in the past. Governments have to behave so that expectations are fulfilled and the trustworthiness of the currency is maintained. I think this is quite different from war. I would therefore use 'competition' to describe the non-system that we have. If we criticize free-floating and volatility, we have to form a judgment about what the alternative would be. What would be the exchange rate that could be supported in the long run?

Back to the point I made yesterday, let us assume we have one world currency: which places would be expensive, in terms of purchasing power parity or in terms of a price index; which countries would be cheap? Newly industrializing countries would be cheap compared to countries that have less development potential. Countries that suffer from long-run disadvantages would have low land prices and low prices of locational factors that are attractive, including labor. This international competition for capital in the long run is one of the stabilizing factors of a non-system.

PAUL VOLCKER: I am perfectly happy to allow a lot of short-term volatility in your terms, it is the medium-term that I am concerned with. Let me tell a little story that I think illustrates the problem. When I was teaching a seminar at Princeton a few years ago, students and the young professor who was working with me kept telling me, "we want to see a real live speculator." So I said, OK, I'll produce a real live speculator, and I took George Soros down there when he was at the height of his notoriety. This was the only time that most of the Princeton economics faculty appeared at my seminar. George was in great form, and he started off by saying that the concept of equilibrium that dominates economic thought has no relevance to the [foreign] exchange markets. Just forget about it. You won't make any money if you think about equilibrium so try to divorce any thought about equilibrium from your mind. All he's worried about is where the market is going to go the next day and what the expectations are in the market. I made feeble defenses of equilibrium, and a young professor followed up with a question. He said, "You know much more about trading than I do, but Mr. Soros, you underestimate the analytic work that economists are doing and the progress that we're making in the a field called chaos theory" [equilibrium models that produce highly irregular time series]. That seemed to me to characterize the present state of analysing exchange movements [as totally unpredictable]. None of the other Princeton faculty said a word, and seemed unimpressed with Soros's knowledge. And they never attended another one of my seminars.

Returning to managing volatility in the short run and long run, some kind of a target zone would probably encompass what happened to the euro. My conception of a target zone would not encompass what happened to the yen and the dollar recently, but if the euro were about to rebound, that would be within my target zone.

RICHARD COOPER: I just want to make two observations. First, in response to Herbert Giersch, I think it is the case that in any dynamic economy there is going to be an irreducible amount of uncertainty. That cannot be avoided. The uncertainty does some damage and we have institutions like insurance to take care of that, but we cannot eliminate it. We can spread it around, but we cannot eliminate it. The academic argument for flexible exchange rates is that it performs a "damage reducing function" [moves the uncertainty among different parties to a transaction] in a world of inevitable uncertainty and change. Bob [Mundell] alluded to this yesterday. Under certain assumptions like nominal wage rigidity you can show that flexible exchange rates are actually welfare enhancing [makes society as a whole better off]. These are the models that economists usually use. Conversely, the George Soroses of the world make money by guessing day to day or quarter to quarter movements [in exchange rates] because they play in the forward market. I think as analysts we have to entertain the possibility that that process can be uncertainty generating, rather than uncertainty cushioning. This is an empirical question. My observation would be that the trend line we are on is that the uncertainty-generating feature of flexible exchange rates is growing much more rapidly than the uncertainty cushioning [trend]. But as I say, this is an empirical question, an issue for investigation rather than pure theory.

7. The role of gold in the international monetary system

Introduced by

Enzo Grilli and Robert Pringle

ENZO GRILLI: We have come to two topics that are important and related to one another in many respects. They pertain to where the international monetary system is going and where it should or it could go (i.e., a reform of the international monetary system). One question is the role of gold: gold as a reference, gold as a reserve, and gold as an asset. The second topic has to do with the international monetary system and what shape it could take: is fundamental reform, as opposed to marginal reform, necessary at this time? If so, why, and with what components? On the future of gold, I wonder if Mr. Pringle would like to set the stage and perhaps give us a notion of where we are from his point of view.

ROBERT PRINGLE: I am glad we have left the sexiest subject to the end of our conference. Gold has long been one of those almost unmentionable subjects in the international monetary system. It has been a kind of conspiracy of silence. Central bankers have not wanted to talk about it because it is too sensitive a subject. It also brings in political considerations which central bankers have been reluctant to discuss. In the US, for instance, it is the US Treasury that decides gold policy, not the Federal Reserve. In other countries it is the central bank that decides gold policy. In either case, it is a fact that selling or buying gold is a political, as well as a purely financial, action. Therefore, central bankers are generally shy to make statements about gold or policy. I would like to say that the past year, however, has been a very eventful period for official holdings of gold. The big event was the "Washington agreement" on gold. This was actually an agreement among European central banks announced in Washington at the time of the last round of IMF meetings, September 26th 1999, where they said that except for sales that had already been decided, the European central banks who signed the agreement would hold on to their gold stocks for the next five years.

Before I say a little bit about that, I would like to talk about the lead-up to that agreement. It is probably the most important official statement about gold since the late 1970s when the IMF officially took gold out of the center of the international monetary system and tried to put the SDR [Special Drawing Rights, a settlement currency created by the IMF] at the center. Leading up to that there was a series of central bank sales of gold that started to change the image of what would happen to gold in the official sector. The number of these sales should not be exaggerated. The market tends to produce loose statements saying that all central banks are selling gold. In fact, this is not at all the case. There were only six central banks that sold significant amounts of gold over the past ten years. But there has undoubtedly been a change of attitude of central banks regarding their gold holdings. These central banks included Belgium, the Netherlands, Australia, Argentina and Canada, all of which sold significant amounts of gold in that period. The Swiss national bank also announced plans to sell quite a large amount of gold when the necessary constitutional and political procedures had been completed.

In May of 1999, we experienced a totally unexpected bombshell in the gold market, when the Bank of England announced that they would be selling, over the next few years, the majority of British gold stock. This really hammered the price, because people said, if England is selling [its gold], the country of the old gold standard, what will happen next? Subsequently, the gold price went to very low levels, around $252 an ounce. This move was not popular with many central banks outside the UK as the value of their gold stocks eroded. At the same time the IMF planned to sell some of its gold stocks to finance debt relief for certain heavily indebted low-income countries. The Swiss plans for large gold sales were also in the background. This lead to a very bearish outlook for gold with market analysts saying that all 30 000 tons of official gold could come onto the market. Central bankers started to become concerned. There were a lot of private meetings that resulted in the statement which I referred to earlier during the IMF meeting last year in Washington. I'd like to briefly review the main points of that statement.

First, the signatory central banks (the central banks of the EMU area, plus Switzerland, the UK and one or two other smaller central banks) said that they believed that gold would have an important role to play as a monetary asset in the future. That was a very important statement by itself for such central banks to use. Second, the signatory central banks stated that they would not enter the market as sellers over the next five years, with the exception of already decided sales. Those sales would total 2000 tons during this period. The market quickly made allowance for the planned sales.

Equally important to the announcement on sales, however, was the announcement on lending policy. One of the aspects that had driven the gold price down in the last few years was the increase in net lending by central banks of their gold stock that added to the supply of metal in the market. The signatory central banks said that they would freeze lending and operations in derivative markets in gold over the period of the agreement. I was officially briefed by a spokesman for one of the [European] central banks who said that although the United States had not signed the agreement for legal reasons, US policy is not to sell gold and not to lend gold either. The Bank of Japan also associated itself with the agreement. So between the big European holders of gold and the biggest holder in the world, the United States, and other big holders associating themselves informally with that agreement, this took 80–90 percent of official gold stocks out of the market, except for the amount that they had already approved. The amount that they approved to be sold over the next five years was 2000 tons – 400 tons a year – which is not much above what central banks had been selling before and this amount can be absorbed by the gold market because demand for gold for jewelry around the world is well in excess of new mine production. As a result of this statement, the gold price shot up, probably more than some of the central banks had thought it would, and has since settled down around $280–300 an ounce. So central banks and governments took action to stabilize the market and to calm down fears of huge central bank sales.

There are a lot of questions that remain after this. Was it essentially a defensive move by some central banks worried that more central banks wanted to sell? Was it just propping up the situation for the short term? Or did it reflect a desire by some European countries to hang on to gold for the longer term, not just for the next five years (especially France, but also other European countries)? The market is asking: what will happen after the end of the Washington agreement?

Because there is only some 4000 tons of gold outside this agreement altogether, most people expect considerable movement of gold stocks in the longer term, both among the countries who are not part of the Washington agreement, and eventually among the Washington agreement signatories themselves. Smaller countries have tended to sell gold stocks in the past few years, and larger countries have tended to hold on to their gold stocks.

Another issue is the longer-term future of gold in the system. The exchange rate stability that Professor Skidelsky spoke about yesterday is one aspect, but another aspect is the use of gold as a reserve asset. What gold holdings will we see in the world? Many observers expect smaller countries that are pegging to a larger country like the United States or the EU, to question the need for gold. For example, Argentina, Belgium, and the Dutch sold gold when they were effectively pegged to the D-mark. I expect that such smaller countries, when they are free to do so, will sell gold, but for large countries to continue to hold onto it. Why is this? Most governments and central bankers still believe that gold is an element that supports the credibility of a currency. In Professor Giersch's eloquent statement about currency competition, gold could be a weapon in such currency competition in the long run.

ENZO GRILLI: The floor is open. The question really is whether gold is going to disappear as a reserve asset, or if it maintains a role, what role and why? Is it because of tradition, credibility, or usefulness?

CHRISTOPHER JOHNSON: There seems to be a kind of inertia about the way gold carries on as a mandatory reserve. One might complain that its value is so volatile that it is even worse than holding yen, dollars, or euros as reserves. The price of gold can fluctuate even more than the price of those currencies in terms of each other. However, we have now what is really going to be a two-currency world system across the Atlantic. I deliberately leave the yen out because it has shrunk as a reserve currency; it is not a currency most countries want to hold in their reserves. So what we have is a remarkable two-country, two-currency model where the US has euros and some yen admittedly in its reserve, and the EU has dollars in its reserves. Some people might say that this is an act all done by smoke and mirrors, and ask: with two currencies supporting each other, what is supporting them?

The classic economic answer is the strength and low inflation of the US economy and the rather smaller European economy. There is an argument saying that one reserve underpins both these world currencies and that is gold. If you look at how much gold there is in reserves, the ECB has 15 percent of its reserves in gold at market prices, and the UK has about 18 percent. All euro-land countries still have a lot of gold left in their reserves because their own euro reserves were wiped out once the euro became a domestic currency, so they just have dollars and gold. The proportion [of gold] in national reserves varies from 35 percent in Germany to 51 percent in Italy with others in between. The US has more; it has about 56 percent of gold in its reserves. However, there has been an argument put forward by French authorities who state that the ECB should have not 15 percent, but 30 percent gold in its reserves. This could occur if the European members of euro-land were to pool all their reserves.

Let us consider a world with euro-land that has 30 percent gold in its reserves and the US with just over 50 percent. Does this make any difference? Does it increase the confidence of small countries in the Far East that these currencies are underpinned by something? Should we all enter a conspiracy that believes gold is an important monetary asset? Or should we draw aside the veil and say the emperor has no clothes, that gold is a useful commodity, and sell it and devote the money to canceling the debts of developing countries? That is an idea that the IMF has played around with. So it seems to me that there are quite a lot of options, but we should not create too many illusions around gold.

MAX CORDEN: I have a simple question. Why should any central bank voluntarily hold gold when it earns no interest?

RICHARD COOPER: At an earlier stage in life I had some responsibility for making decisions about disposals from the strategic stockpiles of the United States. During the 1950s the US built up a stockpile of crucial raw materials in preparation for the possibility of fighting World War III. Fortunately that stockpile did not need to be used, and the nature of war changed so dramatically that this became a historical anachronism. The question arose as to how to dispose of these materials, storable goods that go into war production. The disposal issue came in a period in which the US budget was in substantial deficit and selling off some assets was a good way to reduce the rate of increase of the public debt. It will not surprise you to learn that every producer in the world came in to oppose the disposal of these stockpiles. It was straight self-interest. They benefited, collectively, from the build-up of the stockpiles during the 1950s when demand exceeded supply while the stocks were being built. But, of course, they objected strongly to the disposition of the stockpiles.

I think that this agreement on gold, which we just heard about, has to be interpreted in the same way. The sale by Australia and the Netherlands, which signaled that at least one traditionally gold-oriented central bank – the Netherlands – had changed its view completely on gold, followed by the announcements of others, represented the possibility of a heavy disposition of gold. That was not only of concern to the producers of gold, but also to the other holders of gold. This is a common phenomenon where there is excess capacity and low marginal costs; for example, the airlines face this problem in pricing their seats. I think it was perfectly rational for central banks, in their own self-interest, to agree to moderate the sales of gold, because it was not in the interest of any of them to see the price of gold drop to a hundred dollars an ounce. I actually see this as a cartel in action, and I think that putting a monetary spin on it is based on the hopes of all those who would like to see a continued monetary role for gold. If I had been in the meeting when the agreement was discussed, I would have voted for it, but I probably would have voted for three years rather five years. I was a little surprised at the five-year moratorium.

I have exactly the same question that Max [Corden] raised. I think there is no benefit [to central banks] in holding gold. When I have a complicated financial question like the role of gold in the [international monetary] system, I try it out on my cousin who farms the old family farm in Kansas. He is an absolutely superb farmer, but does not know anything about finance, although he sees through all of this. As long as authorities can set the price of gold, gold performs no discipline on the system whatsoever. We ought to be upfront about it, we are inevitably in the hands of judgments of people like Otmar Issing and Paul Volcker when he was at the Fed. We put our hands, and I think correctly, into the hands of wisely chosen people to determine our monetary affairs for us. We do not need gold. Gold plays no useful role, and my cousin the farmer sees that completely intuitively without understanding all of the analytics of it.

ROBERT MUNDELL: With respect to Dick Cooper's comment, it should not come as a big surprise to us that people do things out of self-interest. Economics is based on that [idea] and it is the basis of a free market economy. The relevant issue is the role of gold in the international monetary system, if there is a system. That role was very important in the Bretton Woods arrangements. The Bretton Woods arrangements broke down in August 1971 because the US did not have enough gold. Since then, there has been no international monetary system. So it seems to me that the question about the future of gold turns on whether or not we go back to an international monetary system.

In the history of man, since coinage anyway, 2700 years ago, gold or silver has always been a part of the international monetary system. Since 1971 it has not been part of the system in any particular sense. The IMF still prices the SDR at 1/35 of an ounce [of gold], so gold has not completely disappeared from the books. The official price is kept there. During the 1970s, the IMF and the [US] Treasury were selling gold and trying to destabilize the gold market. They wanted to make it unstable because the international authorities had decided that they would ease gold out of the international monetary system. Then the price of gold shot up to $850 an ounce in February 1980, instead of going down when they were trying to sell it. But not a single central bank wanted to sell at $850 an ounce. Then, last year the Bank of England wanted to sell gold when it was at a low price. Why should central banks sell gold when it hits bottom and not at other prices?

I gave a lecture at the Bank of Italy in 1983. The price of gold had gone down from $850 an ounce to $300 an ounce, and I started off my lecture commiserating with the Bank of Italy at the tremendous loss in the dollar value of their major asset: gold. Nobody knew what I was talking about. The relevant issue is that if we go back to an international monetary system five or ten years from now, will gold be part of it? If gold is not going to have any function, then it would be in the interest of countries to get rid of it. But, would I recommend to the US Treasury that they sell their 250 million ounces of gold? The answer is no. Would I recommend that the ECB sell off some of their gold? I think that they probably have more than they need so in the long run they should. I think by and large that central banks should do what they want with gold. They should think about the prospects for gold in the future, whether it is going to be good or bad for them, and maximize the returns on their portfolios like it is any other asset.

I would like to hear whether Dick [Cooper] and Max [Corden] would recommend that the US and Europe sell off their gold stock.

RICHARD COOPER: I can answer factually because I did recommend in the 1970s that the US sell its gold stock. Because of the stock-flow problem, the rate at which these sales take place is very important. I was not interested in losing money for the American taxpayer, so the sales had to be at a moderate rate. I claim responsibility for the IMF sales in the mid 1970s, having persuaded Henry Kissinger that this was a good way to deal with the oil shocks. I would recommend this now, but at a measured rate. I would absolutely not dump it onto the market.

ROBERT MUNDELL: Would your target be a zero level of gold reserves?

RICHARD COOPER: Like all of us, I have a finite life and I actually believe in leaving some decisions to the next generation. I would sell at a rate that maximized expected revenue and then I would leave the remaining gold stock to be decided by the next generation.

PAUL FABRA: I want to make a few remarks to make the discussion fair. When we speak about gold there is so much emotion and ideology, and usually the discussion is unfair. I think two or three basic remarks have to be made to achieve that goal.

First of all, I would like to say a few words about what I call the "Triffin fallacy." I was a great admirer of [Yale economist] Robert Triffin, but I think what he said about gold was wrong. Within the national boundaries of any country, gold has disappeared as a means of payment and money is now used. So the natural evolution of the international system should be the disappearance of gold as a means of payment between nations. But I do not agree to use the usual jargon, that "progress is money that is more and more abstract." I think we have a confusion of concept. Money is never abstract. Money is purchasing power. The problem is how do you measure, or how do you maintain, the purchasing power of money?

Today, we have replaced the reference, namely gold, by an index of prices, or rather a basket of commodities and services in the form of the index of prices. We say that the dollar or other currencies are stable in terms of their purchasing power of a basket of commodities and services. The difference between the two systems is that in the gold system one can judge the purchasing power of the money in the [gold] market, and today it is much more difficult to gauge that through an artifact, which is an index of prices. The gold standard, by definition, is based upon the idea that there is an essential difference between money and credit, and that has something to do with the concept of liquidity. In a gold standard economy, money is equivalent to a certain quantity of gold, gold being the liquid asset, the ultimate form of purchasing power. The question raised by Max Corden (why does a central bank bother with gold because it does not pay interest) is completely irrelevant. In a gold standard, money is by definition the liquid asset and should not yield any interest. The advantage of an asset that yields no interest is liquidity.

ANDRÉ SZÁSZ: A lot of the emotion that was originally attached to the issue of gold that we have just heard has gone out of the subject. I do not think it is the most important subject we face. If I were a present-day central banker, I would have a certain reluctance to sell gold for three reasons, two of them practical. One has been mentioned, its effect on [gold's] price. The second concerns the complications that may arise from maximizing profit [from gold sales]. I can imagine that not everybody would agree with me about what to do with the revenues from gold sales. Why cause complications if they are not urgently necessary? Bob Mundell has already alluded to the third argument: we do not know the future of the [international] monetary system. I have some doubts about a monetary union between the United States and EMU as was mentioned yesterday. Because of these issues, one cannot exclude a future role for gold.

ROBERT BARTLEY: Let us imagine that the Federal Reserve or the ECB decided to stabilize their exchange rates, and one currency was at the top of its [agreed upon trading] band and the other currency was at the bottom of its band. The question arises as to where the burden of adjustment would be. We have to have some judge of whether one country has been to tight [with monetary policy] or the other country has been too easy.

In the current situation, there would be an argument about whether one [country's] consumer price index is better than the other. I can envision a role for some monetary indicator outside of the system as a guide to which central bank has to adjust. Gold has been a pretty useful monetary indicator over the last 20 years or so. It did not get up to $850 [an ounce] for nothing; it got up to $850 because the Fed was inflating. When the Fed started to tighten, it went back down. Paul [Volcker] said that he should have tightened sooner in 1987. That is when gold was rapidly increasing again; it got up to about $400. [US Treasury Secretary] Jim Baker got into an argument about which country should adjust and we had the 1987 market crash. The following January, central banks jointly intervened and the markets recovered. Gold during that period seemed to serve a pretty useful role as a monetary indicator. I used to be monetarist but now I am looking at gold [as a monetary anchor]. Gold does not seem to have worked as well recently, perhaps because of central bank sales or because we are out of an inflationary environment. But, I can conceive that in a monetary system with exchange rate bands, it could again become a rather handy indicator.

MANFRED NEUMANN: We should simply ask ourselves, what the purpose of gold was during the last 25 years. After the breakdown of the Bretton Woods system, there was no purpose except one: serving as collateral. There was one case where Italy used gold for collateral in the 1970s in order to get an international loan. That was the only purpose I can remember over the last 25 years. If central banks wanted to keep their gold stocks that would be a signal to me that they do not trust the future course of their policies. That is, they need some collateral. I think it is rational to sell small amounts. In Germany we have a politician who writes a big article every year in the newspaper about selling the gold stock, and every year he has a different idea of what to use the money for. If you sell too much on one occasion, then it is tempting for governments to spend [the revenue] on idiotic things.

MARIO BALDASSARRI: My question is the following: what are we looking for? I think we are looking for something with two characteristics: maintaining purchasing power over time, and generating profits. Since we live in a global market, why not have an SDR related to a world equity index? What is better than this in terms of value in time and profitability and the lowest risk possible on this planet? But if we have a world crisis, we could have a crash in the world equity index. And what could be a shelter? It could be gold.

ROBERT PRINGLE: First, you can lend in gold. You can lend gold as a central bank at 1, 2 or sometimes 3 percent, which is as much as you get on yen, for instance. Second, there is the question about what you do when you sell gold. The British government is investing it in euros, which have sunk by 10 percent since they began. Gold has a role as a diversification instrument. Mathematical economists have shown that it is beneficial to have gold as an element in a diversified portfolio because the gold price is driven by fundamentally different factors than currency prices. Additionally, it is insurance against extreme states of the world, and several speakers have referred to possible extreme states. One of them is a resurgence of inflation in reserve centers. There is not any inflation now in major reserve centers, but who knows what will happen in 20 or 30 years' time.

Third, gold has an amazing record of maintaining its real purchasing power over centuries in a way that no currency has done. Of course, if you invested in Wall Street for the past 20 years, you would have done much better than gold, and some central banks, I'm sorry to say, are beginning to invest in Wall Street. I think gold is probably better.

8. Fundamental reform of the international monetary system: necessity, timing and future directions

Introduced by

Enzo Grilli

ENZO GRILLI: Our next topic is based on the following question: is it time for fundamental reform of the international monetary system? There are several themes that have emerged from our discussions. To begin with, is reform really necessary? Some would say that systemic instability would indicate that we need reform. Others would say that efficiency requires it. Are there better systems than the current non-system? If so, is the EU currency area a path towards a new system?

Second, is reform of the international monetary system feasible, given the number of countries? We have talked about Europe, Japan, and the United States, but the number of [other] countries is very large. There are a variety of preferences expressed in the choices of exchange rates. There are a variety of preferences expressed in terms of the policies. There are a variety of situations regarding openness. Therefore, the question of feasibility should not be forgotten.

Third, if there is fundamental reform, is a common exchange rate regime desirable? If not, are there principles for going to a better system of exchange rate regimes than the sort of free-for-all system that we have grown accustomed to? The choice of exchange rate [regime] is important not only for the countries that make them, but also important from the standpoint of the general stability of the system. Therefore, some judgment on those choices is desirable.

Finally, is there a role for the IMF [International Monetary Fund] in either keeping the system of exchange rates compatible, or rather should its role be confined to other areas, for example, as lender of last resort? There are a variety of proposals regarding the role of the IMF, and there is the position of the Fund itself about its functions. All this and more is fair game.

MAX CORDEN: It seems to me there are two problems with the present system. One is the instability of the exchange rates between the yen, the dollar and the euro. The second problem is the instability in the international capital market that would also exist with a fixed rate regime. The movement from euphoria to panic severely destabilizes many developing countries. Now how is that to be dealt with?

One solution is to control it. One objection to control is that there are so many ways around it, including leads and lags, multinational companies fiddling around and so on. If one does try to control it, there are major disadvantages. Still, this is one possibility.

Another approach is to argue that it all has to do with information. If people, who go from one extreme to the other, understood the difference between, say, Asia and Latin America, or knew where Indonesia was, or had studied economic history at business school, they would not go to such extremes. Then, if the IMF and Bank of International Settlements provide them with more information, people will act more sensibly. It turns out that a lot of the information has always been available; most people just did not get around to reading it. Still, that is one approach.

The other approach is to accept the instability of the private sector, which is something that Keynes wrote about a lot, and to let the IMF and governments acting in cooperation compensate for the instabilities. In reality, there will always be herd movements, panics, and euphoria, but one view is that the IMF and the governments standing behind it have more sense than the private sector. This is an ideological question, because maybe they do not have any more sense, maybe they are all in the same boat. But if you think there is some role there, then you want a strong IMF.

Lastly, I'll open up another topic. A new commission, the Meltzer Commission [chaired by Carnegie Mellon Economics Professor Allan Meltzer], has recently reported for the US Congress on the IMF. If the majority of that commission gets its way, we will hardly have an IMF, and will certainly not be in a position to do any short-term lending to deal with these inevitable instabilities in the private sector. But there are really big questions here. Does the private sector always get it right? Is it self-correcting? Does the government always get it right, or get it wrong?

RICHARD COOPER: In Max [Corden's] taxonomy, I fall into the third category, although I am not sure I would characterize it in just the same way. I do believe that private financial markets are intrinsically unstable. In terms of securities markets, we heard earlier about the importance of benchmarking. Benchmarking, in fact, is irrational. The reason benchmarking is important is that the ideal situation for any financial institution is to do modestly better than the benchmark and one's competitors. Not radically better, because that usually involves taking greater risks. So I think that financial markets intrinsically involve herd behavior; the incentive structure is conducive to herd behavior. Therefore, it is the public's responsibility to minimize the real economic damage, not the capital gains and losses, but the real economic damage that can be done by herd behavior.

I share the concerns and anxieties that have been expressed in this conference by Bob Mundell, Paul Volcker, and others. I think that flexible exchange rates have served an important role historically, but I think they are going to become more and more costly as time goes on. Therefore, I would look for serious reform of the monetary system and I actually think that a currency union among the major industrial democracies, by which I mean the EU, the US, and Japan, is a good idea in the long run. I have no illusions about the political feasibility of such an arrangement anytime in the future, so I set it twenty-five years from now. But I think it needs to be actively discussed, the pros and cons, the institutional arrangements that are non-trivial, although I think they are not insuperable. That is a longer-term vision. The question is what might be reasonable next steps?

Here I revert to something I alluded to yesterday, although the details differ in important ways. It is now fairly common practice for central banks to target price stability. The character of the assignment, its formality and so forth, differs from one country to another. It is much tighter in Europe than it is in the US. It is tighter still in Canada and New Zealand. But it leaves open the question of what price index we are talking about. The usual assumption is that we are talking about the consumer price index [CPI]. What I want to suggest is that I think that is a bad idea. The appropriate price index that we should be targeting, having in mind the broader framework of the international system, is a good wholesale price index, rather than the

138 *International Monetary Policy after the Euro*

consumer price index. If all of the leading central banks successfully targeted the wholesale price index, they would, in fact, be targeting approximately the same target. Keynes actually made a comparable proposal in the *Treatise on Money* in 1930. He had an index of 62 internationally tradable commodities and he suggested that that be the target of the central banks. Of course, he was writing in the context of the gold standard so that proposal is irrelevant now. But I think some modern variant of it actually makes a lot of sense now. That is what I want to leave on the table as a transition to at least the possibility of a monetary union in the future. I would have the central banks target what is approximately a common index to deal with some of the problems that we talked about earlier.

The difficulty with this approach is transition. We know from historical experience that the consumer price index tends to rise over time in stable advanced countries. That does not occur with the wholesale price index of tradable goods. So the operational recommendation that I make this afternoon is that we ought to rethink the object of monetary policy targeting and shift away from the consumer price index to the price of tradable goods and services (I do not mind including services as long as they are tradable).

NORBERT WALTER: Richard, would you help us to clarify whether your wholesale price index is a three-year moving average or do you allow for business cycles effects. Secondly, if you allow for the price development in the tradable goods sector, are you aware that services in tourism, and more importantly, services in the high-tech area are damn difficult to measure. How do you deal with that?

RICHARD COOPER: On the last point, the answer is unambiguously "yes" in principle, but these are practical difficulties that have nothing to do with the international system. We have a terrible time domestically pricing these services. As I said yesterday, there are serious measurement problems in our domestic price indexes. That is especially true of new goods and services. So there are all kinds of practical problems, and where the practical problems become too difficult to solve, you leave them out. But conceptually they should be in.

In terms of [business] cycles, I would follow a "leaning against the wind" strategy, which is a strategy that central banks that target prices do follow. If the CPI moves 10 percent above the ceiling, they do not instantly drop the money supply by 20 percent. Wholesale prices will vary, and I would follow a tracking policy. I would not formalize it in terms of a three-year average, but I would follow some sort of loose tracking policy. For better or for worse, we are all in the hands of the judgment of the collective decisions, in the United States, of the Federal Reserve Board and the Open Market Committee [that sets US monetary policy], and in Europe, the ECB [European Central Bank]. I would give the best economic analysts possible to these bodies, give them their general objectives, and then let them do their work. I don't know if *ex post* this would be consistent with using a three-year average, but I certainly would not advocate this going in. But on the other hand, I would not react sharply to any deviation from the target either.

ALEXANDRE LAMFALUSSY: I have another question. You first used the expression "internationally traded commodities," and then you came down to internationally traded goods and/or services. What is the role of commodities in your index? Your wholesale price index includes what exactly?

RICHARD COOPER: I did not mean number two. Operationally I would take today's extant wholesale price indices.

ALEXANDRE LAMFALUSSY: Domestic prices?

RICHARD COOPER: Yes. They differ of course, but they are dominated by internationally traded goods. That is the way I would start. Then I would have international discussions about which items might be dropped or added to those goods. I think I would end up with an index of relatively homogenous manufactured goods, that is to say they are not crude oil, but number two fuel oil, for example, which is a relatively homogenous product, electrolytic copper, steel of a certain quality and so forth, so that semi-manufactured goods would dominate the index. There would still be CPI inflation and that goes to the setting of the target. With this kind of index, I think a target of zero, rather than 2 percent might well be appropriate.

PAUL VOLCKER: I will try to summarize reform of the international monetary system briefly. I will accept as a proposition the inherent instability of private markets. I would add another assumption that financial globalism is here and will continue and be intensified, which among other things makes it very difficult to apply controls consistently over a period of time without really insulating an economy in a way nobody wants. There are two problems that jump out that need attention. One is the instability of exchange rates, and particularly exchange rates among the major countries. But, under any conditions, I think small countries have a big problem living with the combination of circumstances I have described – the inherent instability of private markets and globalism. In particular, there will be too much money moving too fast for a small country with an inherently small financial system to absorb and diffuse without a proclivity toward repeated crises. We have seen a lot of that in the past even without extreme globalism. I really think small countries cannot exist in this situation with any degree of stability. Obviously we cannot do away with the countries, so what do I mean?

I think that more financial systems need to be foreign owned. The way they are going to get stability is borrowing size and diversification from a larger institution, which involves international ownership. We talk about all kinds of reforms and strengthening local supervision and all that stuff. What is happening is that these banking and financial institutions are being bought by other banks, much bigger banks, that consider themselves stable. I think that is inherent in this situation.

Let me make a small aside by saying I think most of the reaction to the crisis in Latin America and Mexico [in 1994] was not irrelevant. It is very convenient for us in big countries to say that they ought to have strong banking systems, well supervised and transparent, American accountants, GAAP [generally accepted accounting principles]; none of the responsibility is ours, it is all theirs. To overstate the point, I think it is completely irrelevant. I used to supervise banks that went bad and I know that it is not very easy. I would like to take the example of contrasting Texas in the early 1980s with Indonesia or Thailand in the late 1990s. Texas in 1980 was considered to have the strongest banks in the US. They were well capitalized, highly profitable, they were dead-set against interstate banking because they did not want anyone else coming into their territory where it was so profitable, they were well supervised, at least by American standards. I was one of the supervisors, so I feel particularly strongly about that. They adhered to GAAP accounting, they had American accountants, and they had transparency. They also had an oil boom, which led to a real estate boom. Five years later there was not a big Texas bank that was solvent and half the savings and loans were bankrupt and gone. This occurred in the good "ole US of A." That led to unfortunate circumstances in Texas and they had a difficult time for a couple of years, but they did not have a collapse. Why didn't they have a collapse? Because there was no question of currency instability, we were using the dollar. There was no question of 40 percent interest rates, because they had American interest rates. So they had a difficult economic period, but they did not have anything like a major crisis that their counterparts in Asia [Thailand, Indonesia, Hong Kong, and their neighbors, 1998] or Mexico [1994].

When I get to the big currency [management] problem, I would like to think there is a halfway solution. I admit it is very difficult. What I have in mind is a very wide target zone, at least plus or minus 10 percent, maybe plus or minus 15 percent. If you do not like to call it a target zone, I could even think of something more informal. I think it can be managed. The trick is to have some credibility in the system and then encourage stabilizing speculation instead of the opposite where you get wide swings. How you get the credibility is the problem. I think our earlier discussion showed how difficult that is. Unless governments are convincing about their willingness to protect it, including using monetary policy, you can forget about it. And you get all these interesting questions about who takes the action, who is the umpire, the numeraire of the system that we discussed earlier in the context of gold. I am not going to answer except to say it is very difficult. I used to think the wholesale price idea was good. I still do not rule it out, partly because you can speculate in goods. You cannot speculate so easily in services and they are much harder to measure. So if you could really stabilize wholesale prices, you can stand a small creep in the services prices that you cannot measure very well anyway. This is not so easy because goods are becoming less important [in national accounts] than services.

I would conclude by mentioning the difficulty in managing, and getting credibility, in a relatively loose target zone system. In the end this requires a strong IMF that can be the umpire and help determine where the equilibrium rate is, loosely defined; who is responsible for moving where; bringing public and private pressure and all the rest. If you do not have some kind of body to intervene in the inevitable arguments between the Europeans, the Americans, and the Japanese about who acts when, you are in trouble. These are not very happy days for a strong IMF, so I recognize there are certain problems in getting my little vision implemented. But it should be easier than jumping all the way to monetary union between the United States, Europe and Japan. And it is deliberately designed to leave some elasticity in the system for some independence of monetary policy, maybe even in some circumstances enhancing the independence of monetary policy if you really knew that you had sustainable limits, rather wide limits around the exchange rate.

VÁCLAV KLAUS: I would like to say a few words about the IMF as well, more about the IMF than about the international monetary system. To simplify the situation, I would like to say that my perspective is very much different from Paul [Volcker's] perspective because he starts by saying there is an inherent instability in private markets. I would start with a totally different proposition, that there is destabilizing behavior by the IMF. Maybe the destabilizing behavior of the IMF is not that big, because there is definitely a huge gap between the real relevance of the IMF and its nominal importance. I think the real relevance is visibly much smaller than what is nominally discussed and debated. I dare to say this because I brought my country into the IMF, I signed all the documents as Minister of Finance and I was the Governor for Czechoslovakia in the IMF for three years, so I think I can discuss these things. But looking at it from our perspective, what is the IMF? For us it is another rating agency. It is another potential source of funds for a country, on the condition that the country needs them. Finally, it is another advisor or consultant. You have many competitors in those three fields and I would say that the IMF is not the best one in any one of those three. For example, my country had needed money at a point in time, and we repaid the standby arrangement six years in advance without touching the money. We discovered that there is no need to ask for money from the IMF, because there is plenty of money in the world and it is not necessary to finance the trips of IMF officials from one continent to another.

As an advisor or consultant, I must say that there is an enormous deteriorating tendency in the quality of advising. With the huge increase of IMF member countries, there was a visible deterioration of quality of the missions which have been sent into my country and other countries. I remember the first missions in 1990; this group of people were of high quality. Another problem is the very frequent shift in fashions of ideas, opinions, and recommendations as if nothing happens. I remember in 1990, I tried to introduce flexible exchange rates, because I was afraid that with liberalizing prices and foreign trade after 50 years of totally frozen prices, there could be many chain reactions that I could not imagine. I was so afraid to set the exchange rates at the beginning. I tried to convince the IMF to keep it floating and then after several weeks, we will see how much the prices moved and then we may do something. Impossible! We would have been excluded from the IMF for not accepting their fixed exchange rate regime.

I remember in 1997 when our mini-crisis started, everyone was saying it was a mistake to have a fixed exchange rate, so why didn't we move to flexible rates in advance? The high real interest rate policy, a very popular recommendation by [Deputy IMF Managing Director, 1994–2001] Stanley Fisher, is now remembered as a terrible mistake. This is another problem which I really feel is a serious story. I would prefer to have a weak IMF, not a strong IMF. In this respect we may be on the same side of the barricade to minimize the role of the IMF permanently, if not to privatize it.

PAUL VOLCKER: Just to clarify my view, we are talking about different aspects of the IMF, and I share many of these questions about the IMF being all-seeing, and all-knowledgeable in dealing with its clients in small countries. I was talking about a role for the IMF that has almost been forgotten as an arbiter among the big countries, an entirely different role where they do not need a lot of lending and they do not need a lot of economic advice, but they may need an arbitrator. I am not sure that they are a good enough or strong enough arbitrator, but somebody has to arbitrate.

ENZO GRILLI: The more I hear about the IMF; the more I think it is the Holy Ghost. Everybody claims to have seen it. Everybody claims to have seen it with a different robe. Everybody claims that it is too powerful. I wonder if we see shadows or if we see realities – I was not referring to you Mr. Klaus, I think you saw reality as far as the Czech Republic was concerned. But I wonder if we really are not talking about very different things here. I would like to stick to the notion that the IMF is a useful, fallible, and serious organization.

ALEXANDRE LAMFALUSSY: I would like to make one point about privatization. If you look at what the private rating agencies did in the case of Asia, they produced the best lagging indicators of an imminent financial crisis. [Editor's note: many of the Asian countries that faced financial crises in 1998 were predicted by members of the 1997 Bologna–Claremont Monetary Conference.[4]]

NORBERT WALTER: One could argue that Europe may develop towards an "euroization," and the Americas towards a dollarization, and these have a clear structure. I have no idea what the structure is for the third pillar. We have been talking about the yen, and this normally would translate to the reference point being Japan. But we all understand that this is wrong. But at the same time, I have not seen any alternative idea about the Asian financial market and the Asian exchange rate regime. Nobody mentioned the suggestions made by the Hong Kong Monetary Authority about an Asian monetary union. I would be very interested to hear from those who have grand ideas or designs for the world currency system as to what they believe Asia will look like in the tripolar world.

MANFRED NEUMANN: I think the answer to the question of whether we need a new international monetary system should be made empirically. Several participants have said that the private sector is unstable. But if you read the history of the world monetary system over the last 50 years, then the hypothesis that policies are unstable has some support. I hold that most large fluctuations came from bad policies; they may have been strengthened or made larger by the financial market reaction, but the source I point to is government. If this is correct, it seems to me it would be more important to reflect on international rules for policies. For example, do independent central banks need clarification of what we mean by price stability? Also, why not have some type of rules of conduct of fiscal policies? That would help a lot, because it would imply that if countries would sign such an agreement, hopefully policies would become more stable, at least among the larger countries. This would be useful.

Additionally, Paul Volcker talked about a target zone system with the IMF playing a role. This is not as much of a straightjacket as a new Bretton Woods system would be, but we already have a floating system, so why don't we start with Europe and the US. We could have some informal arrangement between the US and Europe and see how it works out. Before we could do that, we would have to verify who in

4.   See Zak, Paul J. (ed.) *Currency Crises, Monetary Union, and the Conduct of Monetary Policy: A Debate Among Leading Economists*, Cheltenham, UK and Northampton, MA, USA, Edward Elgar, 1999.

Europe could negotiate with the US. That is completely open. We have the Maastricht Treaty. It would say the European Council can make the decisions, but it can only make the decisions with the support of the ECB [European Central Bank]. So this first needs to be clarified in Europe, and that is a long way away.

ENZO GRILLI: This is the famous Kissinger problem – who do I have to call in Europe, what's the telephone number? We still have that problem.

PAUL VOLCKER: I will accept that that would be a good way to start. But let me overstate a point because I think there is some reality to it. The idea that good policy is going to cure this problem with small countries I think is wrong. An example in the early 1990s was Mexico. Everybody thought it was terrific, and there were a lot of good things there. They got so much money it killed them. The same thing happened to a considerable extent in Asia. I think there is a structural problem here that cannot be cured by good policies for small countries. The basic point is the imbalance between the size of their financial systems and the international markets. I am sorry to keep repeating this, but I was startled myself that the Tequila Crisis [1994 crisis that began in Mexico] went down to Argentina. Going there, it suddenly sank in that the size of the Argentine banking system (and the banking system is pretty much the financial system), was 45 billion dollars, which at that time was the size of the second largest bank in Pittsburgh, Pennsylvania.

ROBERT MUNDELL: We did not get to talk much about emerging markets. One thing I want to say is that there is a big movement in Latin America and some other areas of the world to form their own currency areas. The EMU has had a demonstrable effect. For a long time these countries have been told that they should float and not do anything about fixing, and then they see the eleven countries in Europe not just fixing, but scrapping their own currencies for a common currency. That idea is catching. So you have all kinds of proposals in Latin America for a Latin American dollar, for dollarization, maybe "euroization," and more interesting, backed by at least prospects in Brazil and in Argentina, the idea of a common currency for Mercosur. I do not know how the arrangements for that would work out. But one thing that is clear is that given the volatility of the international monetary system, and the fiasco that has surrounded the appointment of the managing director of the IMF [Horst Köhler], the IMF has lost a lot of prestige. If there isn't some movement to reform, then reform is going to be carried out in the periphery. The peripheral countries want a better deal out of the international monetary system, and I think they deserve to have it.

In this conference, I think we have come a long way. There is an evolution of opinion. A few of us, at least, have come to the idea that fixed exchanged rates are not a completely half-baked idea. It is something that might eventually emerge in the future, if not in our lifetimes. One thing we do agree on, with maybe just a few exceptions, is the idea that for each country the primary consideration [for monetary policy] is certainly price stability. As Keynes insisted in 1923, the primary consideration is price stability, but a secondary consideration is exchange rate stability. While Keynes mentioned [exchange rate stability] as an important secondary consideration, I think that it is becoming close to being a primary consideration because of the interconnectedness of financial markets. When we think of many of the financial transactions today, instability of exchange rates is a very bad idea. I just cannot imagine a big stock market like in the US suddenly split up among three currencies. A common currency would be a wonderful benefit. It would be a step forward at least if the major currency areas could change their view from clean floats and benign neglect toward the view that it is worth making some investment in exchange rate stability or reduction in exchange rate volatility.

MAX CORDEN: I wanted to supplement some remarks that Paul [Volcker] made referring to developing countries, particularly the successful developing countries like Thailand and Mexico that get tremendous capital inflows, euphoria, and then panic. He focused on the financial crisis aspect of this, and said one possible solution is more foreign-owned banks. There are ways of overcoming the financial aspect of this. The other aspect is simply the inevitable deep recessions that come at end of the boom. That would exist even if all the banks in Thailand were American or German. That's why I think, with reservations, there is a role for the IMF to provide essentially compensatory finance to tide countries over the recession period so they can have temporarily bigger fiscal expansions.

RICHARD COOPER: I would like respond to Norbert Walker's question and to avoid any misunderstandings. When I talked about a currency union involving Europe, the US, and Japan, I meant Japan the country, not Japan as a proxy for a yen-area in Asia. My view of Japan is that it will continue to be a very important national economy in the world. It is unquestionably in relative decline. And it is in relative decline for demographic reasons. The demography of Japan looks as bad as the demography of Italy, and Japan, as is well known, is extremely inhospitable to immigration. So it is a country in relative decline. I do not see a serious yen-area developing in East Asia for both political and economic reasons. I think the Asian countries, if they orient themselves to some international currency at all, will focus on the US dollar or the euro, not the Japanese yen. So my inclusion of Japan is because Japan is an important economy, not because the yen is a world currency.

9. Randall Hinshaw Memorial Lecture: choosing exchange rate regimes. Lessons from Europe and Asia

Presented by

W. Max Corden

INTRODUCTION

It is an honor to give the Second Randall Hinshaw Memorial Lecture on the occasion of the fifteenth Bologna–Claremont Monetary Conference. Randall was the devoted organizer, fundraiser and, above all, editor for this series since its beginning in 1967. It is with great regret for all of us that he is no longer with us. But this notable conference series and the books that it spawned will always be his memorial.

What kinds of exchange rate regimes can be recommended to so-called emerging market countries – that is, developing and transition countries with open or fairly open capital markets? What are the lessons of recent events? This is currently a hot topic, and just now the academic debate centers on the "hollowing out" proposition: that the choice is inevitably between the two extremes – currency boards or monetary union on the one hand, and floating exchange rates with only modest smoothing intervention on the other. That is a pretty stark choice. In this view, anything in between, notably fixed or adjustable regimes, are discredited, at least for emerging market countries. I want to discuss this with special reference to East Asian countries. What lessons can be derived from their experiences and what suggestions can be made for them?

Thus it is Asia rather than Latin America or the transition economies on which I shall focus. Furthermore, I shall not be concerned with the dollar–yen–euro relationship; but I shall reflect on whether EMU has any lessons for the emerging market countries.

BASIC PRINCIPLES

Before turning to East Asia, a few words on basic principles. There are essentially three possible objectives for choice of regimes and actual exchange rate policy. The first is the objective of exchange rate stability, the implication being that floating rates create undue instability or "misalignments" that are adverse for international trade and capital movements. This is the objective which governed the EMS [European Monetary System] in its early stage, until 1983.

The second is the real targets approach, which sees the use of the nominal exchange rate as a policy instrument to adjust the real exchange so as to attain, together with expenditure (absorption) policy, notably fiscal policy, the targets of internal and external balance, however defined. This textbook approach governed IMF policy recommendations to developing countries in balance of payments trouble right through the 1970s and 1980s. The typical recommendation to a developing country that needed to improve its current account: reduce the fiscal deficit and devalue.

The third is the nominal anchor approach, designed to anchor a country's inflation rate by fixing the exchange rate, or fixing a rate of crawl [vis-à-vis another currency]. This approach governed the EMS, and notably French exchange rate policy, from 1983 and has also been influential in Latin America, notably Argentina and until 1995, Mexico.

THE ASIAN EXPERIENCE: THAILAND

Coming now to the Asian experience, it will help to focus the discussion if I talk at first about just one country, namely Thailand, where the crisis started. Up to the 1997 crisis, the Thai baht was effectively, though not formally, pegged to the dollar. This peg goes back to 1954 when Thailand ended its multiple exchange rate system. There were only two devaluations, both modest in size, between 1954 and 1997, so here is indeed a long fixed exchange rate history. Inevitably, Thailand had very low inflation during the whole of that period. From 1970 to

1989 the per capita growth rate averaged 4 percent. The Thai boom – essentially an investment boom partially financed by foreign capital – actually began in 1987 and only came to an end in 1996. During that period the average per capita growth rate was about 8 percent, one of the highest in the world. I cite these figures of a history of low inflation and high growth to show why it may have been reasonable for some Thais to look favorably on a fixed exchange rate regime.

In the latter stages of the boom, the euphoria stage, many investments were clearly unwise, as evidenced by empty office buildings and housing complexes in Bangkok. A boom mentality pervaded Bangkok. For a long time there was remarkably little real appreciation, essentially because of the plentiful supply of underemployed labor from the rural areas, but eventually real wages did start rising, which reduced Thai competitiveness. For various reasons, including the decline in competitiveness, the growth in exports came to a sudden stop in 1996. In the latter stages of the boom, the current account deficit reached 8 percent of GDP.

Such a boom was bound to come to an end and, given the commitment of the central bank to the fixed exchange rate, was bound to end in an exchange rate crisis in addition to the classic end-of-boom crisis. Then the baht [the Thai currency] was floated. Its depreciation initially overshot, but finally there has been a net nominal and real depreciation. The beneficial effects of the depreciation, improved competitiveness and hence higher exports that both improved the current account and compensated for the loss of employment caused by the ending of the boom, were slow to develop. Hence, inevitably, there was a severe recession. This was reinforced by the financial crisis caused, at least in part, by the accumulation of foreign currency denominated debt by financial institutions.

The question is: would the story have been different under a different exchange rate policy or regime?

The Thais might have adhered to the fixed-but-adjustable regime, but devalued substantially once it became evident that the extent of capital inflow, and hence current account deficit, could not be sustained. That would have been in 1995 or 1996, and was the IMF's advice. Perhaps a large enough devaluation would have been credible in the sense that no further devaluation would have been expected. But given the scale of foreign currency denominated debts, it would have precipitated the financial crisis which happened in any case later. And the financial crisis may have set off a further exchange rate crisis.

But there is a contrast with Latin America. Problems of anti-inflation credibility, or of the danger of a wage–price spiral being set off by a devaluation, would surely not have arisen in the Thai case. This is then the alternative of maintaining the exchange rate regime but making a timely adjustment.

Alternatively, the Thais might have floated the baht earlier. The obvious advantage compared to what actually happened is that the central bank would not have made losses in trying to sustain an unsustainable exchange rate. But there might still have been a sudden depreciation as lenders and the foreign exchange market realized that the boom was ending, or was likely to end, soon. During the capital inflow period there would have been a nominal appreciation, possibly large. Real appreciation would probably have been greater than under the fixed exchange rate regime. On the other hand, there are two novel arguments in favor of floating to which I shall come back later.

Another alternative is a currency board. For Thailand one could imagine a currency board regime to be as credible as that of Hong Kong. Thailand has, or could have, the foreign exchange reserves to back it up, and it has the history of commitment to a fixed exchange rate and low inflation. But would the rate be fixed to the dollar, the yen, or a basket? A basket would make the commitment less visible to the markets. In any case, why is such a straitjacket needed for Thailand? It is the last country where one can say that there is a need for a more rigid nominal anchor: even the recent crisis did not lead to significant inflation.

The principal and perhaps only argument in favor of a currency board is that it would have avoided the sharp depreciation which took place in 1997 and 1998, and which helped to intensify the financial sector crisis. There would still have been a real appreciation during the boom (owing to inevitable money supply growth and price rises), and there would still have been a recession when the boom ended. But any longer-term stimulus to exports resulting from depreciation or devaluation would have been forgone. The necessary real devaluation needed for a medium-term adjustment would have depended completely on the downward flexibility of wages and incomes generally.

I have not exhausted the list of possible regimes one might consider, and will introduce one more later, but let me turn to the "lessons from Europe" for a moment.

LESSONS FROM EUROPE

I have no doubt that EMU will survive, whatever its tribulations. It will be an area of absolute exchange rate stability, with all the conveniences for trade and capital movements that this implies. Hence, whenever there is troublesome exchange rate instability in other parts of the world, people may ask: why not avoid all this and hence move to currency board, monetary union or dollarization? What is good enough for Europe should be good enough for, say, East Asia. Thus the European experience may have a powerful effect on what happens elsewhere. This assumes, of course, that EMU will be seen as a success, especially in Europe itself. In addition, it raises the question of whether there are fundamental structural features that make the euro-land countries plus various potential members different from most emerging market countries outside Europe. Let me briefly turn to these two issues.

First, will EMU be seen as a success? EMU has not yet been put to a test. The kind of problem that has always been foreseen by the analysts of monetary integration, namely that short-term macroeconomic policy requirements may differ between countries, can indeed be seen now. But it is relatively minor. EMU will be put to the test when, or if, there is a major asymmetric shock or, more likely, when there is a major recession and the European Central Bank or the whole system gets the blame, whether rightly or wrongly. The adverse popular judgement of EMU is more likely if the recession has significant differential effects on EMU members. One can also imagine another unpleasant scenario. There may be a strengthening of extreme right-wing forces because of unemployment and, above all, immigration, especially from within an extended European Union. EMU may then suffer from guilt by association. But who knows?

More important for the present discussion are the fundamental structural differences between euro-land and other potential candidates for monetary union or currency boards. The EMU countries are highly integrated in trade, in goods and services. This strengthens the advantages of an area of fixed exchange rates. Furthermore, empirical work suggests that trade integration reduces the strength of cyclical divergences and asymmetric shocks. Speaking broadly, such a degree of integration, so far, does not exist in Asia between Japan, a possible anchor, and other countries, or any other conceivable grouping. For developing countries dependent on a limited number or category of exports, whether commodities, manufactures, or services, the likelihood of asymmetric shocks seems much larger than for any of the core EMU countries. Among major emerging market countries, only Mexico appears to be a possible candidate for integration with the United States. But this draws attention to another special feature of EMU, namely that it is a by-product of a politically motivated movement towards total economic union, and this does not exist in Asia.

TWO NOVEL ARGUMENTS FOR FLOATING RATES

I now come to two novel arguments for floating rates which have come out of reflections on the Asian crisis.

First, it is said that the massive and excessive capital inflow boom was encouraged by the perception that exchange rates would stay fixed. Implicit in this is the thought that floating exchange rates create exchange rate uncertainty, and this discourages capital movements. Presumably it would discourage not just short-term but also long-term flows. Of course, it might be believed that with floating rates long-term purchasing power parity, or something like it, would still prevail. In any case, to repeat, the uncertainty created by floating rates discourages capital flows.

Now, this is a very familiar idea. One argument in favor of fixed rate regimes, and indeed EMU, is that such regimes encourage trade and capital market integration. Fixed rates remove an element of uncertainty. Floating rates create uncertainty. Floating rates throw "sand in the wheels" of capital movements. The question then is whether this is good or bad. Clearly, in the Asian case "throwing sand in the wheels" is thought to be good by some people because, after the event, it appears that capital movements were not always wise. Even if we accept that some capital movements, especially short-term movements, are socially, and possibly even privately, harmful, the deeper question arises whether deliberately creating uncertainty is the most efficient way of limiting such capital flows. I have no simple answer here. In any case, it is paradoxical that the uncertainty effect, which has generally been used as an argument against floating, is now used as an argument in favor.

The second novel argument for floating is that it would induce borrowers to hedge against exchange rate changes. In the Asian countries they did not hedge because they did not expect devaluations or depreciations. And when the depreciations came, holders of foreign currency denominated debt incurred large losses. This was a major factor in the financial crises which devastated these countries. But it is not actually true that markets had zero expectation of devaluation. A Thai firm could borrow more cheaply in dollars than in baht. Presumably the significant interest rate differentials before the crisis reflected a belief that there was at least some risk of devaluation. But hedging is expensive. Borrowers simply gambled that the slight perceived probability of devaluation would not happen, and the gamblers lost. Perhaps they were ill-informed about the probability and actually believed they would be rescued, as indeed to a partial extent some of them were.

Should such gambling be discouraged by increasing the risk, that is, by floating the exchange rate? That is an interesting question. Can it be socially optimal for public policy to deliberately increase risk? Or should the aim be to provide more information or education, both about the possibility of devaluation and about the likelihood (or unlikelihood) of rescue? One could also argue that the likelihood of massive depreciations was indeed small before the event, so that the failure to insure against such an event through hedging was perfectly rational. But now lessons have been learned and, even if countries returned to fixed-but-adjustable regimes, their borrowers will be more careful next time.

THE ASIAN EXPERIENCE: INDONESIA

Coming to other east Asian countries, I do not have time to say much about them, including Hong Kong and its currency board, the People's Republic of China and its fixed rate sustained by high foreign exchange reserves and partially effective capital controls, or Korea with a story somewhat similar to Thailand but not such a history of fixed exchange rates as exchange rates have actually been adjusted much more in the past. Formally none of the countries, including Thailand, have described their regimes as being of the fixed rate type. Supposedly they have all been managed floaters; though in practice they have been (more or less) fixers. In any case, I want to say just a few words about Indonesia. In terms of population, it is a very important country.

Before the crisis, Indonesia had a crawling peg with a band. When speculation against the rupiah pushed the currency to the bottom of the band the rate was quickly floated. No attempt was made to hold the rate, and hence fruitless foreign exchange losses were not incurred. This seemed a perfectly sensible policy. Since the Suharto regime took over, following the hyperinflation at the end of the Sukarno regime in 1965, there had been a long period of very moderate inflation and occasional but substantial devaluations. Thus it was a fixed but-adjustable regime, later becoming something like a flexible peg with a band. There was clearly no need for the exchange rate to act as nominal anchor since monetary bands fiscal policies had been conservative, lessons having been learned from the earlier, disastrous, experience that ended in hyperinflation. Perhaps the situation has now changed, given the new political regime with all its uncertainties. But I doubt that there is even now a strong nominal anchor argument for a currency board.

The extraordinary severity of the Indonesian crisis, to a considerable extent explained by the extraordinary degree of nominal and real devaluation, must, in a deeper sense, be explained not by the exchange rate regime but by the political uncertainties resulting from President Suharto's decline and the inevitable succession problem. That problem was looming in any case. It was impossible to predict how it would develop, and, as it happens, the elderly President (with whom all authority rested) did everything wrong at crucial times. No fixed exchange rate or currency board regime could have survived in that situation. Floating was the only option. Now the country has a managed float. But sentiment in Indonesia is certainly not sympathetic to floating, given the extreme movements in the rate that have taken place. (Before the crisis the rate was 2500 rupiahs to the dollar. In stages it depreciated to 17000 at its peak, and now it is about 7500.)

An interesting reflection is that intervention by, say, the Federal Reserve or the Bank of Japan could have avoided the extreme movements and would have been very profitable for them, as well as somewhat stabilizing.

CONCLUSIONS FOR ASIA

Are there any simple conclusions one can derive specifically for East Asian emerging market countries? "No single currency regime is right for all countries at all times," this is the title of a recent (1999) Princeton essay by Jeffrey Frankel. I agree. But what about the "hollowing out" proposition, to which I referred at the beginning of this lecture?

The argument is that anything between floating and absolutely fixed rates (currency boards, monetary union, dollarization) is not to be recommended whenever a country has high international capital mobility and is either unable or unwilling to control international short-term capital movements.

The distinction must be made between two types of fixed-but-adjustable regimes. First there is the Bretton Woods type of regime: governments or central banks have a strong commitment to a particular rate and want to establish credibility that the rate will be maintained, probably for nominal anchor reasons. That type of regime eventually ends up in major crises, involving first, seriously dislocating rises in interest rates, and finally losses incurred by central banks and loss of political credibility. Beginning in 1976, Mexico has had four crises of this kind. In Asia, Thailand 1997 provides the clearest example. The strong commitment discourages timely adjustment. But such regimes presumably could survive if adjustments were indeed timely. In between adjustments the country would benefit from nominal exchange rate stability. The problem is that in practice, timely adjustments are often not made. Furthermore, speculation may even anticipate timely adjustments.

The other type is the flexible peg regime. It is this regime that I have not mentioned before. This time there is no strong commitment to a particular exchange rate. There is no suggestion that the exchange rate is a nominal anchor. The exchange rate is pegged at any one point in time by the central bank, possibly to a rate of crawl, but the peg is changed when either speculative capital movements or fundamentals indicate the need. This is rather like the EMS operated in its first stage. This regime does make possible some short-term stability of exchange rates. Such a regime seems to me feasible for Asian countries, though it actually comes close to a managed float, and it is close to what some countries have now. But it is still far from the extreme of a floating regime with only smoothing intervention. In the East Asian case, the absence of commitment can be justified by absence of a need for the exchange rate to fulfill the nominal anchor role.

Let me hark back to the three possible objectives for the choice of exchange rate regime, namely the exchange rate stability objective, the real targets approach, and the nominal anchor approach. For many years, East Asian countries prospered with reasonable exchange rate stability. But the real targets approach also played a role. Both Indonesia and Korea made several timely adjustments to prevent or offset significant real appreciations. At times of crises caused by adverse capital market or terms of trade shocks there is a need for rapid real devaluation, as indicated by the real targets approach. Currency boards give stability, at least in nominal terms, but score zero from the point of view of the real targets approach: when capital inflows decline or the terms deteriorate, a needed real devaluation can only be brought about by declines in domestic prices and wages. By contrast, adjustable and flexible exchange rates can be used to satisfy the real targets approach.

On the other hand, currency boards, as well as adjustable exchange rates with strong commitment, meet the needs of the nominal anchor approach. But this approach is (on the basis of recent history) not needed in the Asian cases. In addition, for well-known optimum currency area reasons, currency boards suit small open economies provided they have ample (preferably massive) foreign exchange reserves, like Hong Kong, and are willing to live with all the consequences of occasional severe rises in interest rates. Finally, pure floating rates (with some smoothing) score low on the stability criterion.

When one looks at the recent Asian experience, as also that of Mexico, one must conclude that the fundamental problem is the instability, for whatever reason, of international capital movements: the quick switches from euphoria to panic. When capital flows in, there is an inevitable real appreciation, whether the exchange rate is fixed or whether it floats or is flexible. When inflow stops, or even is reversed, there is an immediate recession in both cases, but such a recession ends more quickly when the exchange rate peg is flexible or the exchange rate actually floats because of the stimulating effects of real depreciation. The real exchange rate and domestic incomes are inevitably destabilized. Instabilities cannot be avoided, but the fixed rate regime moderates real exchange rate instability at the cost of worsening income instability.

As Jeffrey Frankel has written in his 1999 Princeton essay, "No single currency regime is right for all countries or at all times [*Essays in International Finance*, no. 215, (1999) Princeton University Press]." I agree. Thus, I cannot sum up in a single sentence. The best I can say is that for the five Asian countries most seriously affected by the recent crisis, notably Thailand and Indonesia, I am inclined to suggest a flexible peg regime, which is close to a managed float. Pure floating yields too much exchange rate instability, a fixed-but-adjustable regime leads to traumatic crises and a currency board would lead to severe income instability when there are asymmetric shocks.

Index

adjustment mechanisms 9
Africa 6, 17, 73, 94, 102
agriculture 98,
Argentina 22, 102, 83, 103, 125,
    127, 145, 149
Asia 3, 16, 17, 67, 75, 76, 80, 109,
    118, 136, 141, 143, 144, 145,
    147, 148, 149, 152, 153, 154,
    155, 156, 157
asset prices 22
Australia 125, 129
Austria 27, 61

Babic, Mate 13, 96, 98
balance of payments 1, 7, 12, 63,
    73, 149
Baldassarri, Mario 16, 27, 53, 95,
    97, 133
Bartley, Robert 18, 32, 90, 110, 112,
    132
Basevi, Giorgio 13, 14, 34, 87, 93,
    94
Bavaria 62
Bergsten, Fred 76
Bernstein, Edward 3, 6, 7
Blackhurst, Richard 12, 93
BMW 11, 57
Brazil 16, 22, 145
Britain 33, 41, 45, 56, 69, 70, 71, 73,
    74, 80, 82, 100, 113, 114
bubble viii, 17, 19, 23, 53, 77, 119
budget deficits 14, 72, 75, 79, 96
Bundesbank 30, 38, 50, 51, 116
business cycle 49, 79, 83, 138

California 62, 63
Canada 63, 125, 137

capital viii, 2, 6, 10, 11, 12, 13, 17,
    20, 21, 22, 23, 25, 33, 49, 58,
    67, 68, 69, 70, 71, 72, 74, 75,
    76, 77, 80, 81, 86, 94, 95, 97,
    99, 107, 109, 111, 120, 121, 122,
    136, 137, 146, 148, 149, 150,
    151, 152, 153, 154, 156, 157
capital account deficit 12
catalyst 29, 34, 49
central bank ix, 7, 15, 16, 18, 19, 22,
    23, 25, 26, 30, 32, 33, 34, 35, 38,
    39, 42, 43, 44, 49, 50, 51, 53, 54,
    55, 57, 60, 68, 70, 74, 79, 84, 87,
    88, 92, 93, 95, 104, 107, 108,
    116, 124, 125, 126, 128, 129,
    130, 132, 133, 134, 137, 138,
    139, 144, 145, 150, 151, 152, 156
Chile 51
Claassen, Emil 19, 94, 120
Clarida, Richard 47, 48
Clesse, Armand 9
communism 72, 80, 93
competition 18, 28, 29, 32, 33, 35,
    47, 73, 87, 112, 113, 115, 121,
    122, 127
consolidation 15
Cooper, Richard 39, 44, 47, 52, 85,
    106, 112, 130, 131
Corden, Max 52, 65, 66, 129, 131,
    132, 137, 148
corporate finance 12
credit rating 13, 69
Croatia 13, 14, 96
currency
    board 55, 58, 77, 81, 88, 90, 92,
    94, 95, 102, 103, 148, 151,
    152, 154, 155, 156, 157